ABANDONED
EASTERN
CONNECTICUT

ECHOES OF
THE LAST GREEN VALLEY

MATTHEW MEANS

AMERICA
—
THROUGH
—
TIME

America Through Time
www.through-time.com

First published 2025
Copyright © Matthew Means 2025

ISBN 978-1-63499-520-7

Typeset in Trade Gothic 10pt on 15pt
Printed and bound in England

ACKNOWLEDGMENTS

T hank you to Linda, who encouraged an appreciation of history and taught me to seek out the stories behind buildings and places that cross my path. This spark of curiosity has stayed with me from the suburbs of Virginia to the backroads of New England.

A sincere thanks to Colin Theys, for generously providing behind-the-scenes photos from the production of *Dead Souls* and sharing his experiences directing the film.

And a special thanks to John McDonald, for lending his perspective and advice on Connecticut's abandoned mills, gathered from a depth of experience in the field that I can only hope to match one day.

CONTENTS

INTRODUCTION

A drive through Eastern Connecticut is bound to include a myriad of beautiful sights. Around each bend, you'll likely find another quaint village or antique homestead with dry-stacked stone walls, or one of numerous old churches with tall steeples. In between, rolling fields of corn and hay mark the passage of miles and the changing seasons. Yet, beyond this picturesque backdrop is a layer of history that sits slightly in the shadows—a world of dusty gems overtaken by time and circumstance. Often teetering on the edge of collapse or with roofs caving in, they evoke a touch of sadness and mystery, inspiring a natural curiosity about their stories and a desire for elusive answers. Many exist outside the gaze of average sightseers, from derelict houses scattered among the backroads to rustic barns swallowed by overgrowth, each awaiting a seemingly inescapable ruin. Others stand fractured on the banks of rivers—crumbling industrial sites, once corner-stones of local identity, now deteriorating into blights that require vast resources to cure.

These are the forgotten places of the Last Green Valley. Referred to in part as the Quiet Corner, this unique region of the Nutmeg State is home to postcard-perfect towns and pastoral scenery, all wrapped within the only remaining swath of dark night sky amid the coastal sprawl from Boston to Washington, D.C. Encompassed by a National Heritage Corridor that also contains portions of south-central Massachusetts, its record dates back to the earliest days of colonial New England when settlers established an agricultural imprint on the countryside that can still be discerned today. From dairies and orchards to ranches of all kinds, Eastern Connecticut abounds with historic farms and venerable families whose names can still be found on street signs and gravestones throughout the area. But despite a bucolic reputation drawing leaf peepers and joy riders to experience its scenic routes and sprawling parks, the valley also harbors a commercial legacy frequently overlooked by tourists.

In fact, not only do a number of its municipalities feature the remnants of early mills and factories, but quite a few are, to a large degree, a product of those very enterprises. Offering steady employment from the late eighteenth century through the Victorian era and beyond, such industrial pioneers made their fortunes in fine cotton goods and other textiles, fueling economic expansion that lasted for decades. As was the case throughout New England, however, the deindustrialization of the twentieth century saw a steady decline of one-time thriving manufacturers, fostering a patchwork of empty or underutilized buildings. Some remain in good enough condition to repurpose, waiting for hard-to-find buyers with deep pockets and a strong vision. A significant number, formerly the beating hearts of surrounding communities, are left to deteriorate as solemn reminders of lost ways of life.

This book explores a small sampling of Eastern Connecticut's abandoned places— echoes of the farms, factories, houses, and homesteads that make up the fabric of its special character. Occasionally, subjects are identified, while most are left anonymous to preserve their physical integrity, however tenuous that may be (or because they are dangerous locations). Along with a dash of local lore, these pages seek to shine a light on the fading treasures of the Last Green Valley, a timeless landscape shrouded in a rare darkness when night falls.

1

DEAD BUT NOT FORGOTTEN

Eastern Connecticut's beautiful countryside is full of ghosts. With each passing year, time works toward an inevitable outcome for a host of antique homes that sit abandoned and unused, as neglect or expense of restoration prevents these cultural resources from being saved. And so, they exist as "haunted houses," neither here nor fully gone, yet still imbued with a spirit and memory worth preserving.

Here in this gray area between life and death, historical societies, local experts, and the collective consciousness of individual communities strive to pass on knowledge and keep tabs on the remnants in their backyards. Even so, many decaying properties slip through the cracks and only rarely, if ever, come to light again. Among them, very few find themselves resurrected for an unforeseen purpose, let alone a singular use that revives them before the eyes of a wider audience.

It was just such an unlikely turn of events that brought this eighteenth-century homestead back from the grave, courtesy of director Colin Theys and Synthetic Cinema, the production company behind a 2012 horror movie called *Dead Souls*. In search of a derelict property on which to film the tragic tale of a family caught up in supernatural limbo, their team scoured Connecticut for a suitable candidate. Initially casting a wide net, they eventually gravitated toward the Quiet Corner's rural mystique and explored the picturesque country roads of Windham County. What they discovered there was more perfect than they had hoped to find.

The location possessed all the right qualities to make it a great choice for *Dead Souls*: an isolated setting, visible deterioration on almost every surface, and interesting rooms with quirky features that contribute to a memorable and menacing environment. Moreover, it was littered with random furnishings and junk that made for excellent set decoration. It also provided an unexpected coup by offering an antique barn with just the right scale and creepiness the story called for. Sporting an incredibly sinister look, its crow's beak façade lends a distinct air of dread and foreboding to some of the screenplay's most terrifying scenes. And, like the main house, it was also chock-full of grimy artifacts to complete the ambiance. In short, it was an ideal backdrop for a horror film. The director of *Dead Souls*, Colin Theys, noted: "We shoot in a lot of abandoned places. They have a great texture and great feeling … if you want to make something feel abandoned, go someplace abandoned."

Built *c.* 1790, the quaint red farmhouse featured in *Dead Souls* is an excellent example of Cape Cod-style homes of the era and a good match to the picture's fictional Maine locale. Small but comfortable and finely made, even a modest dwelling of this type would have reflected a family with a significant degree of means and status. The building also retains much of its original historic appearance, as does the surrounding landscape, which consists of expansive undeveloped acreage. Unfortunately, in a town full of typically well-documented architecture, information on the original builder seems to have been lost. The property, however, is known to have remained an operational farm until the 1970s before falling into disrepair and changing ownership several times. Sadly, it has ended up in the hands of a commercial enterprise with no interest in preservation.

For all its aesthetic advantages, working here was not without significant challenges. From dust and debris to swarms of insects and an alarming number of dead animals scattered within the basement and walls, there was nothing at all fictional about its abandoned state when the cast and crew arrived. Nevertheless, the place had personality to spare and seemed destined to steal scenes as a de facto co-star.

The house wasn't always the most helpful of cast members, though. Perhaps the biggest headache was grappling with the constricting proportions of the rooms, which in some cases were barely large enough for the actors to perform alongside a single camera operator squeezed into a corner. To overcome the confusion of following movement within these small spaces, the director utilized a wide-angle lens to create an illusion of additional width and depth for viewers. Indeed, balancing a desirable sense of claustrophobia with coherent action is a task that *Dead Souls* excels at. But the inconveniences of filming in an abandoned building didn't end there. Although just a small Cape Cod, it presented oversized challenges to clean up and ready for production, from a grunge-filled kitchen and bathroom to a shockingly disgusting cellar full of jarred mysteries. Even entering and exiting required the use of a power tool to "unlock" the back door.

Colin Theys stated: "I love haunted house movies and I really wanted to focus on the house and the environment and the place … to find the place that would be like a character in the movie."

Here lies the crux of what such an abandoned relic offers during a relatively brief window of time that nothing built-to-order can truly mimic. Precariously balanced between unredeemable ruin and the dim potential of future restoration, the authenticity it affords a movie that calls for precisely such a setting is beyond measure. So, for a short while, a decrepit house valued almost entirely for the land it sits on is transformed into a hidden jewel capable of fulfilling a filmmaker's artistic vision.

Dead Souls may tell the tragic tale of a father's pursuit of immortality, but it also makes for an exceptional time capsule in which to preserve the character of an eighteenth-century homestead—one that sits in perpetual silence along a winding backroad, crippled by neglect, and unlikely to find another starring role anytime soon. Still, a wider audience entertained by the palpable tension and texture it lends to the film's story as a place overcome with shadows and decay, but brimming with history, affords it a final chance to shine. And so, it lives on, dead but not forgotten.

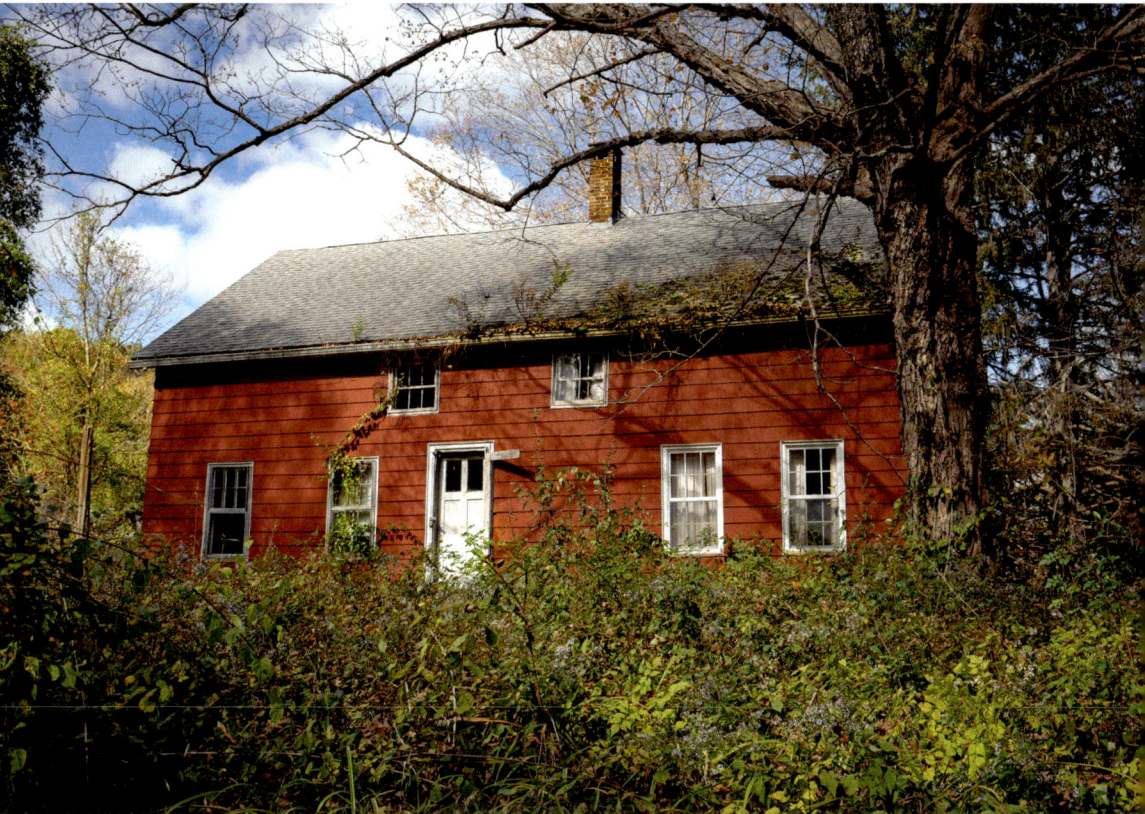

This Cape Cod-style farmhouse has stood here since 1790. Vacant for many years, its red paint job has held up surprisingly well considering the condition of the rest of the building.

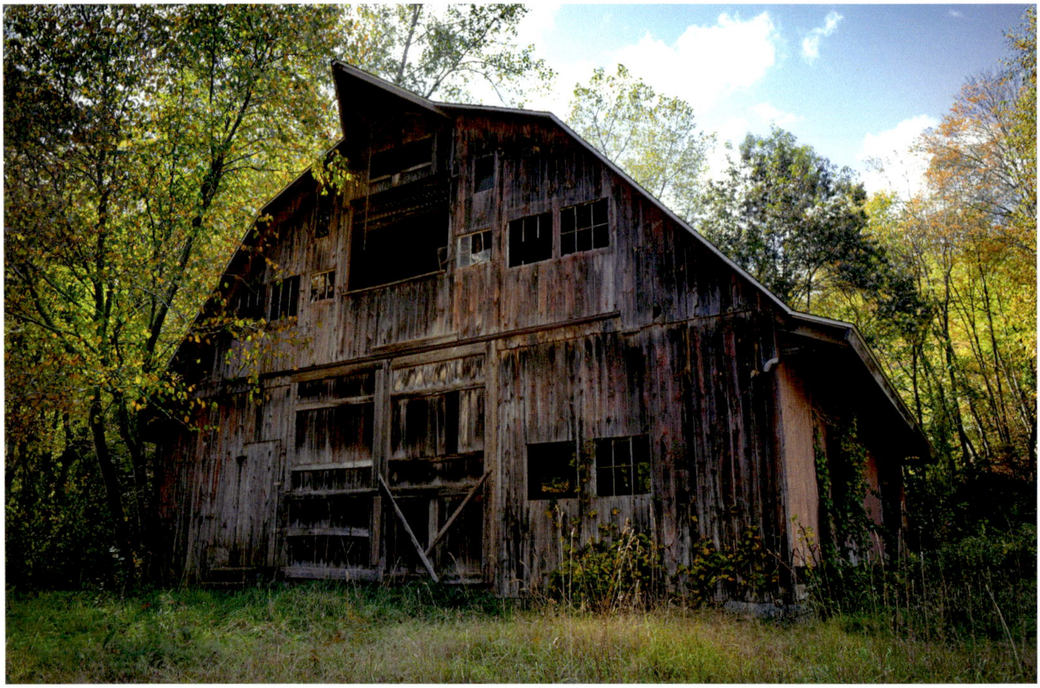

An antique crow's beak barn sits a stone's throw from the farmhouse. Also known as a hay gable, a pointed overhang above the lifting mechanism gives it a sinister appearance.

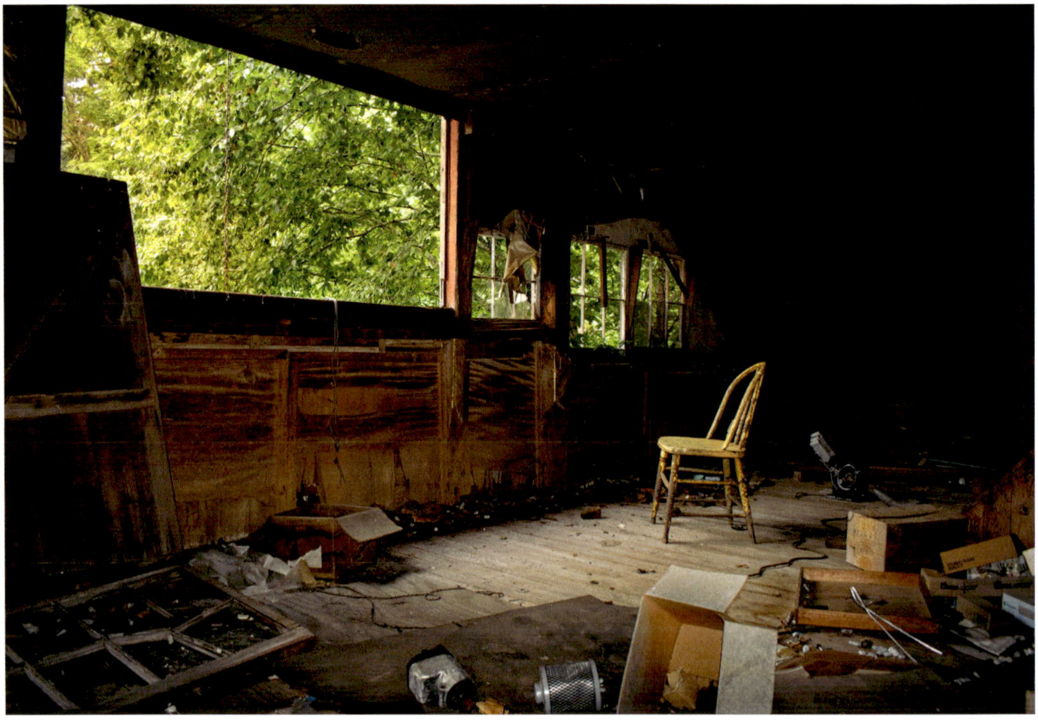

The barn's loft is full of junk, with a mixture of tools, electronics, and trash.

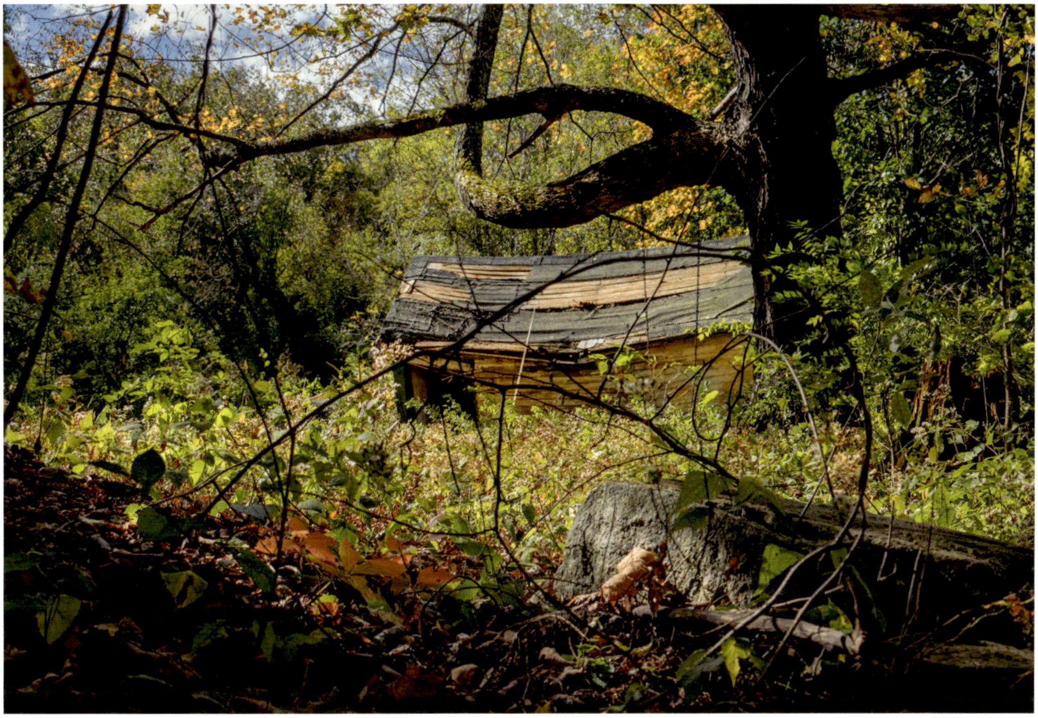

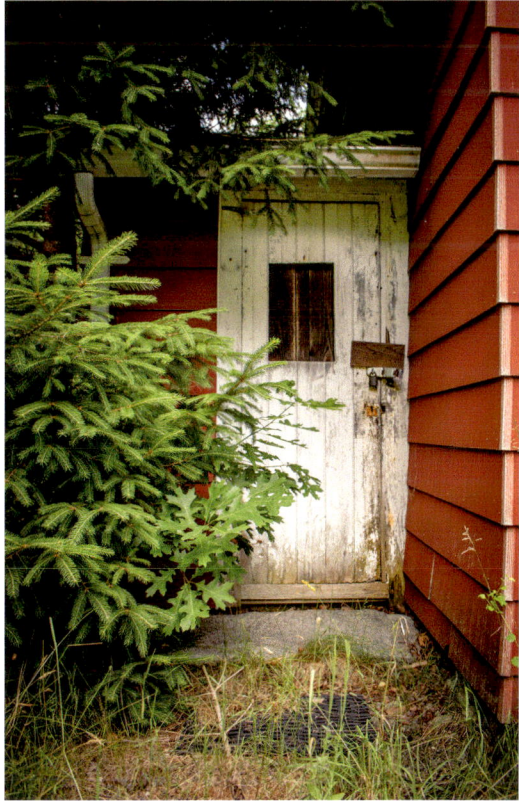

Above: Another derelict outbuilding contributes to the farm's rundown atmosphere but makes for a lovely fall composition.

Right: The crew of *Dead Souls* had to use a drill to open and close the home's rustic back door.

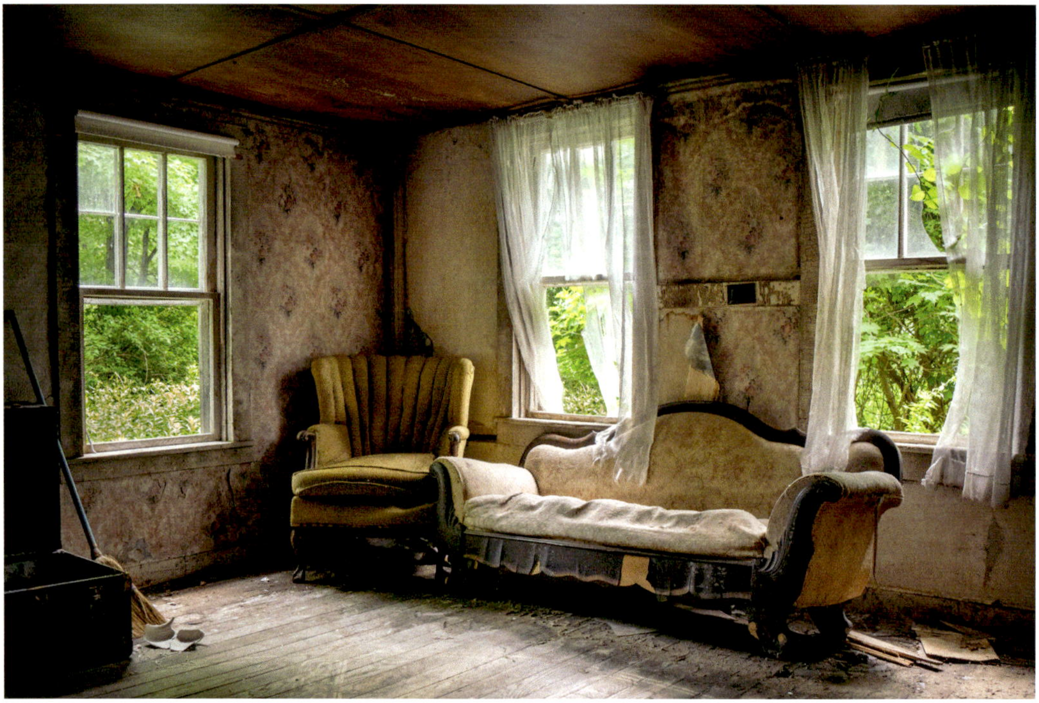

Old furniture deteriorates beneath the house's perpetually open windows. Both the couch and chair were featured prominently in the movie.

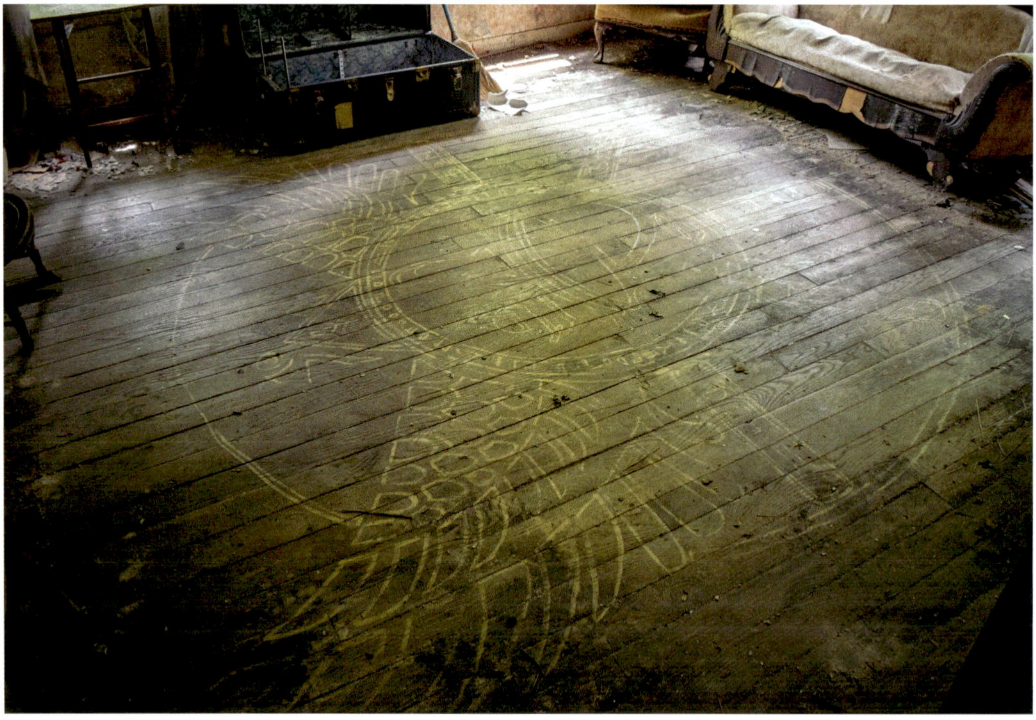

An Egyptianesque ritual circle still adorns the parlor floor—a device the film's characters used in their attempts to conjure ancient magic.

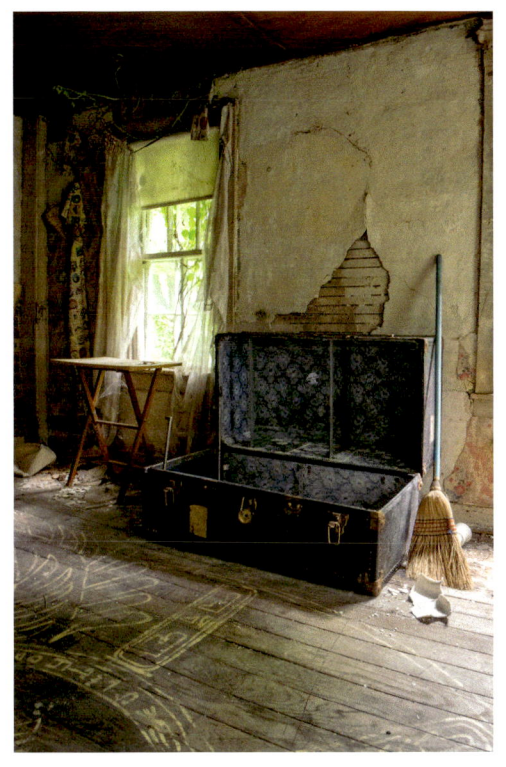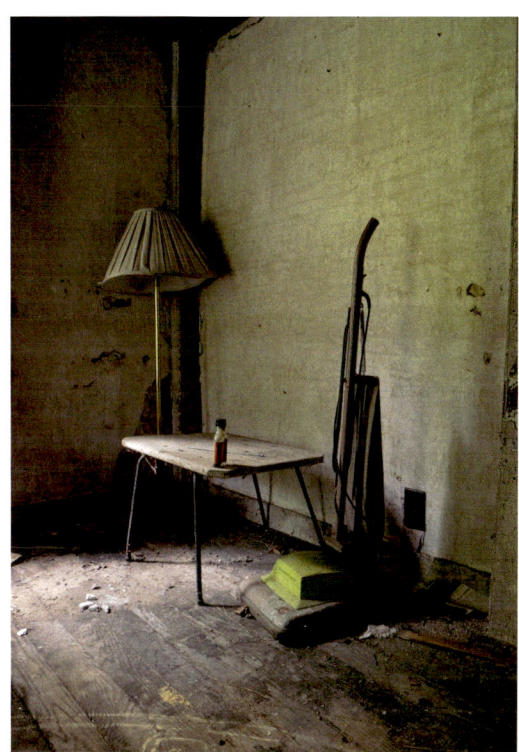

Above left: The lining of a vintage steamer trunk adds a pop of color to the room. Crumbling plaster reveals strips of wooden lath from the house's construction more than 230 years ago.

Above right: A forlorn vacuum shrinks in the corner, perhaps sensing the irony of its presence in this dilapidated space.

Right: Ready for a quiet breakfast on a Sunday morning.

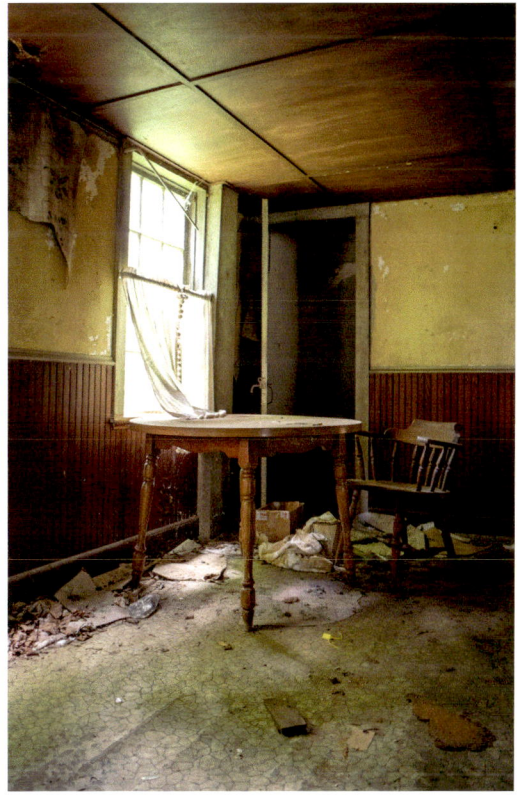

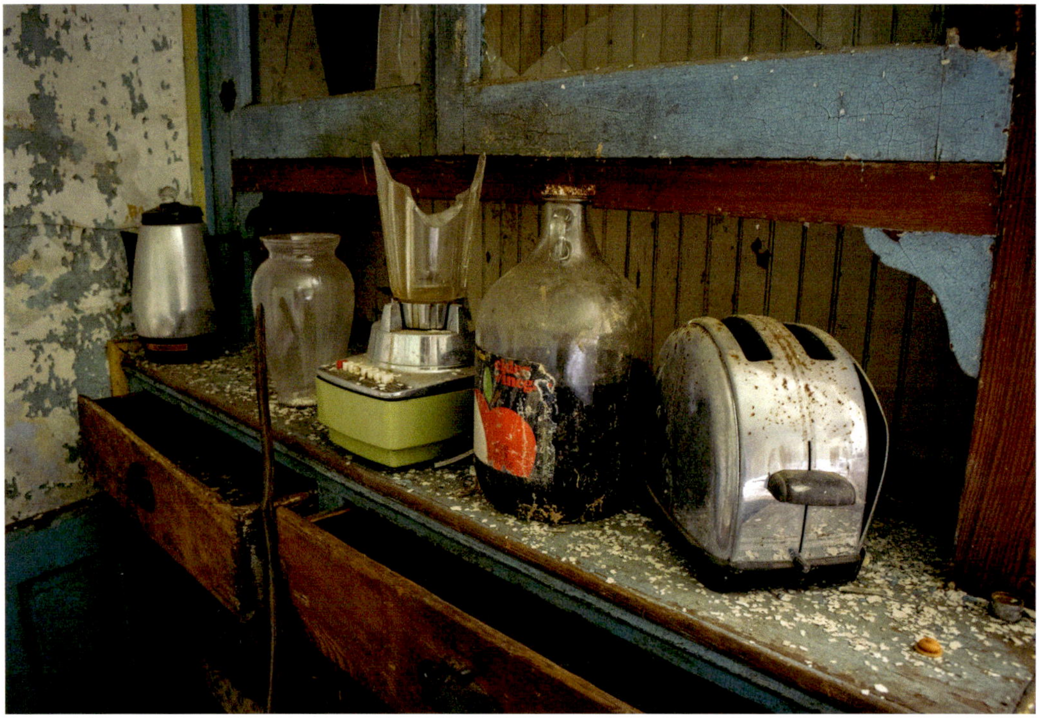

Several damaged appliances, plus a jug full of mysterious brown liquid, are arranged in an almost orderly fashion on this built-in kitchen cabinet.

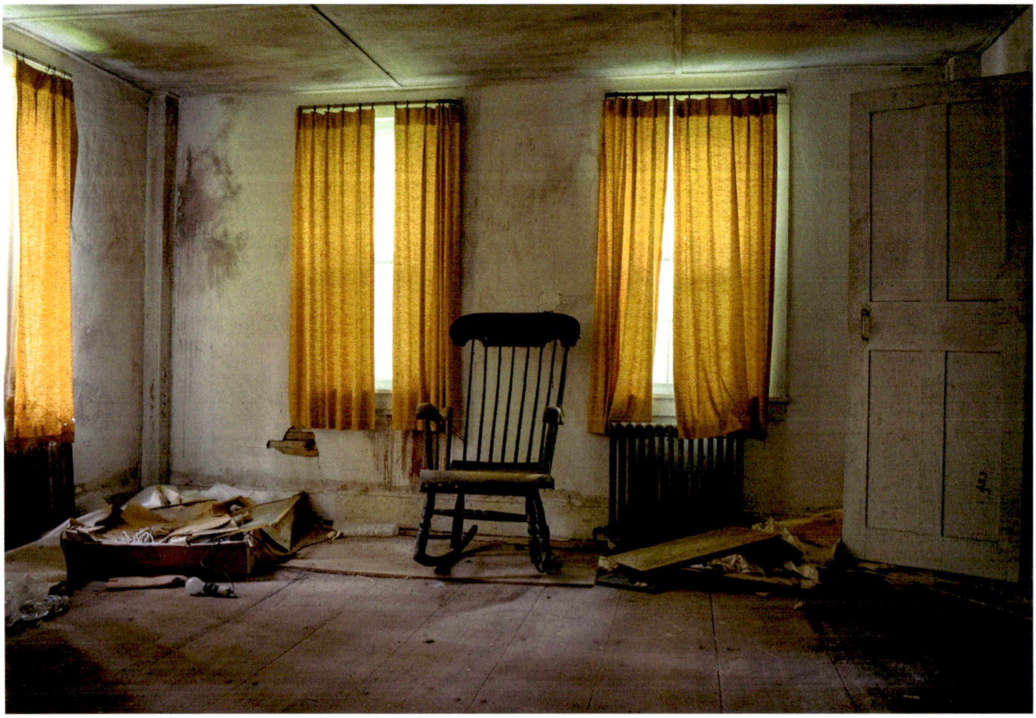

This solitary rocking chair looks ready to move on its own at any moment.

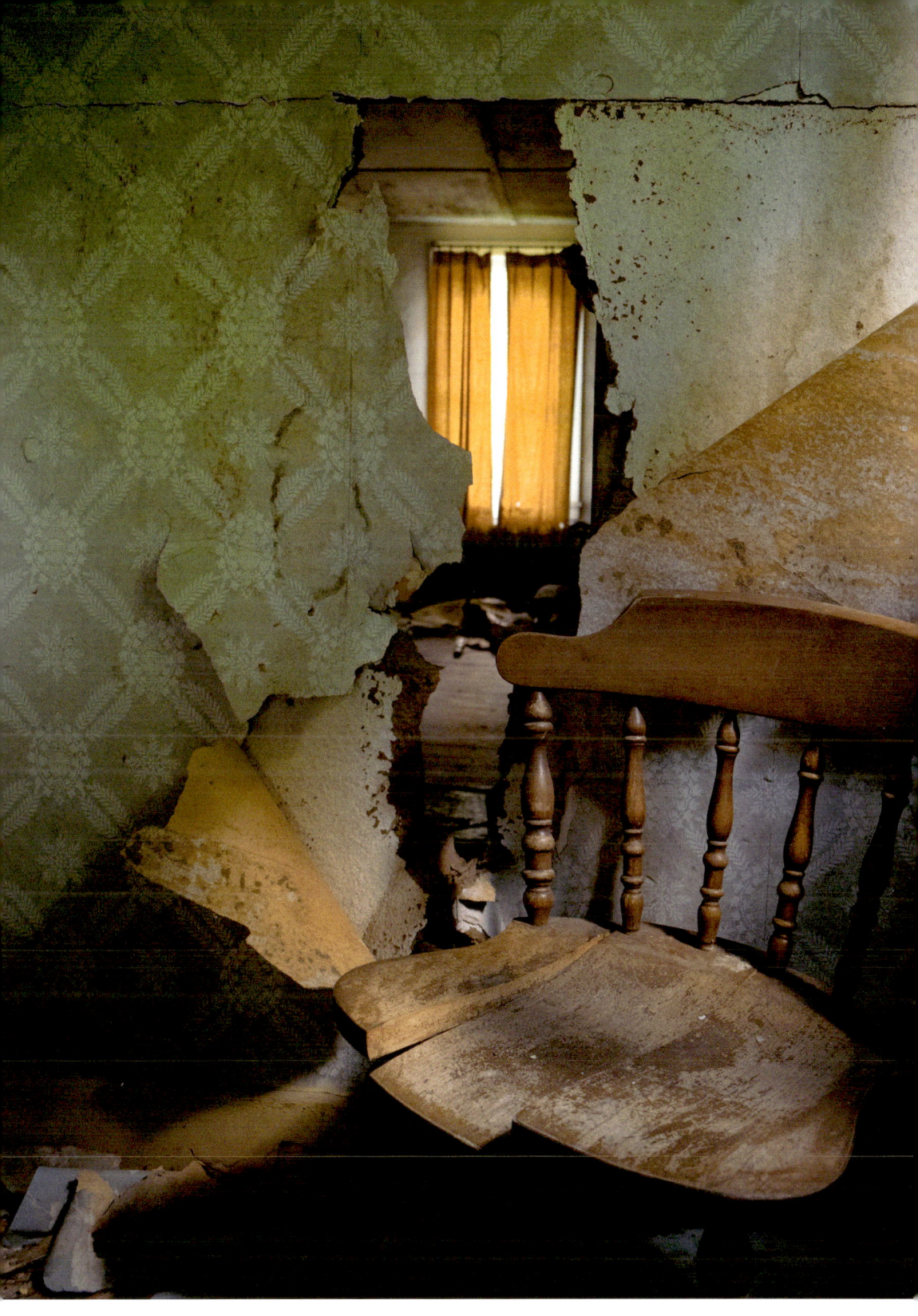

A hole in the wall reveals sunlight streaming through gold curtains in an adjacent room.

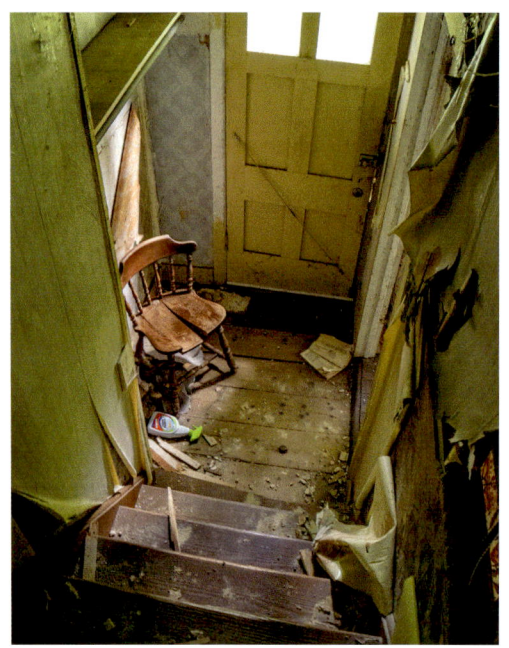 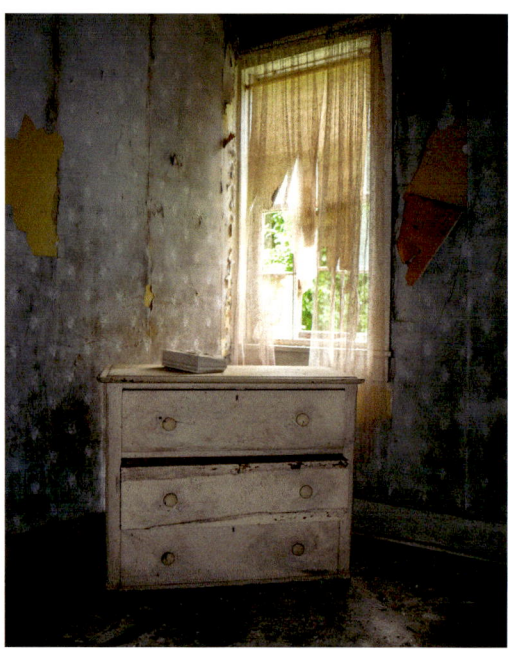

Above left: The central staircase, with its peeling layers of wallpaper, offers a record of the home's decorating history.

Above right: A surprising box of plastic gloves sits atop an old dresser; the how or why of its existence here is a mystery.

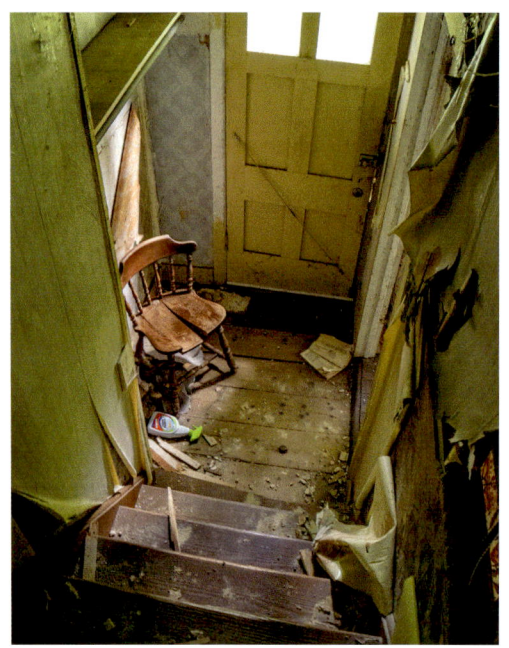

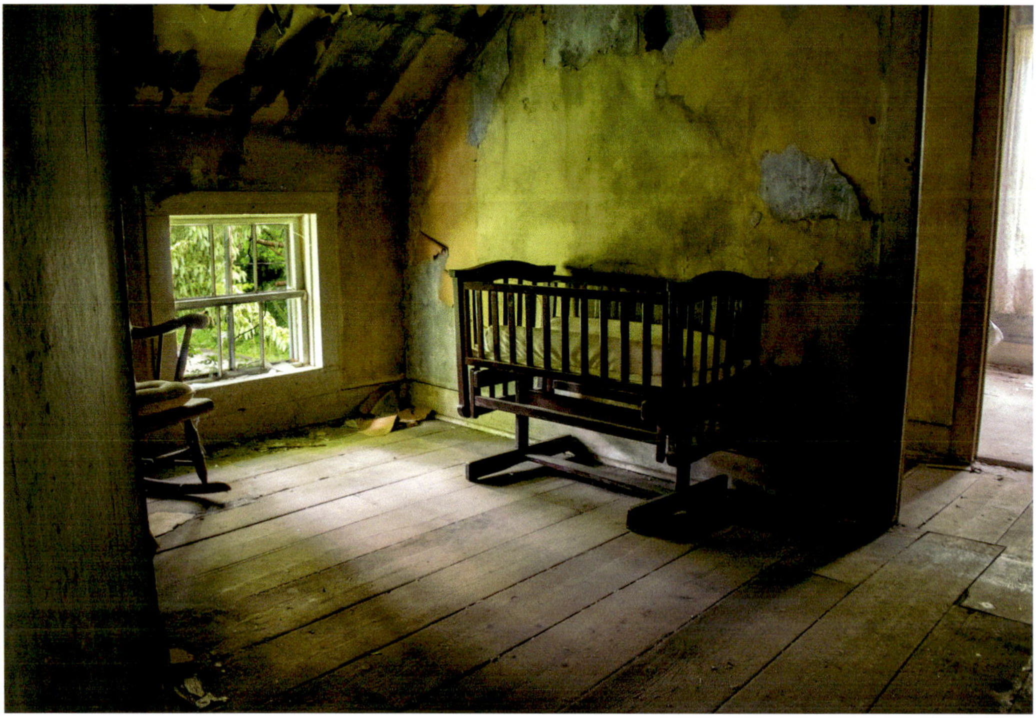

Baby cribs might just be the creepiest category of abandoned furniture. This rocking-style example was left behind after the production of *Dead Souls*.

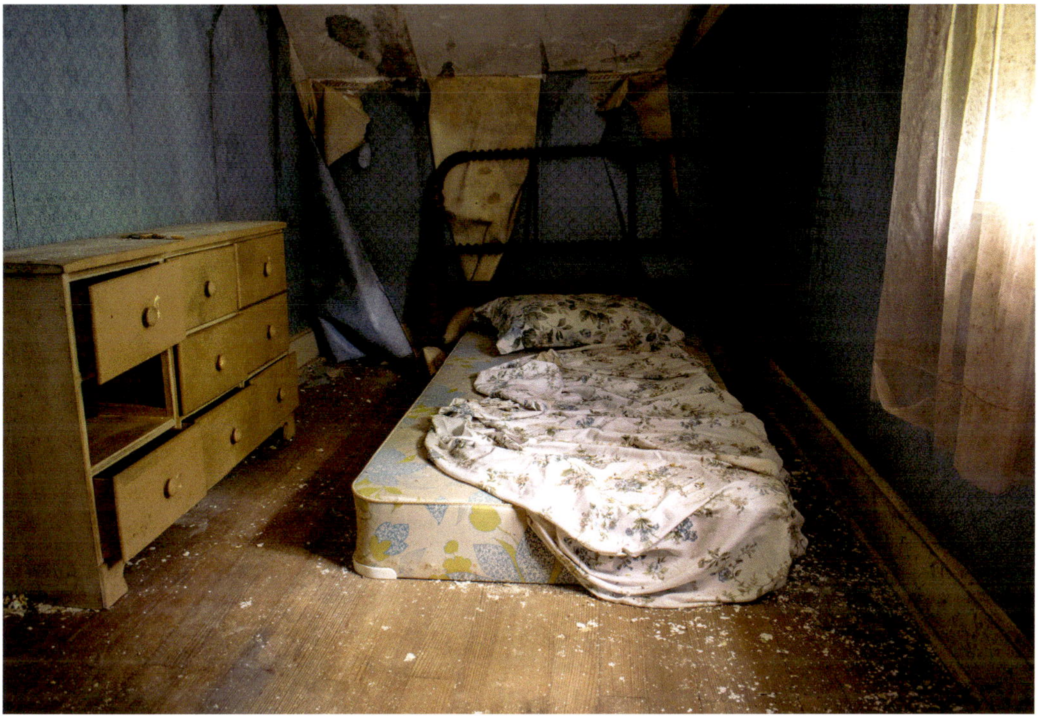

The sheets in this dormer bedroom have made a comfortable spot for resident mice.

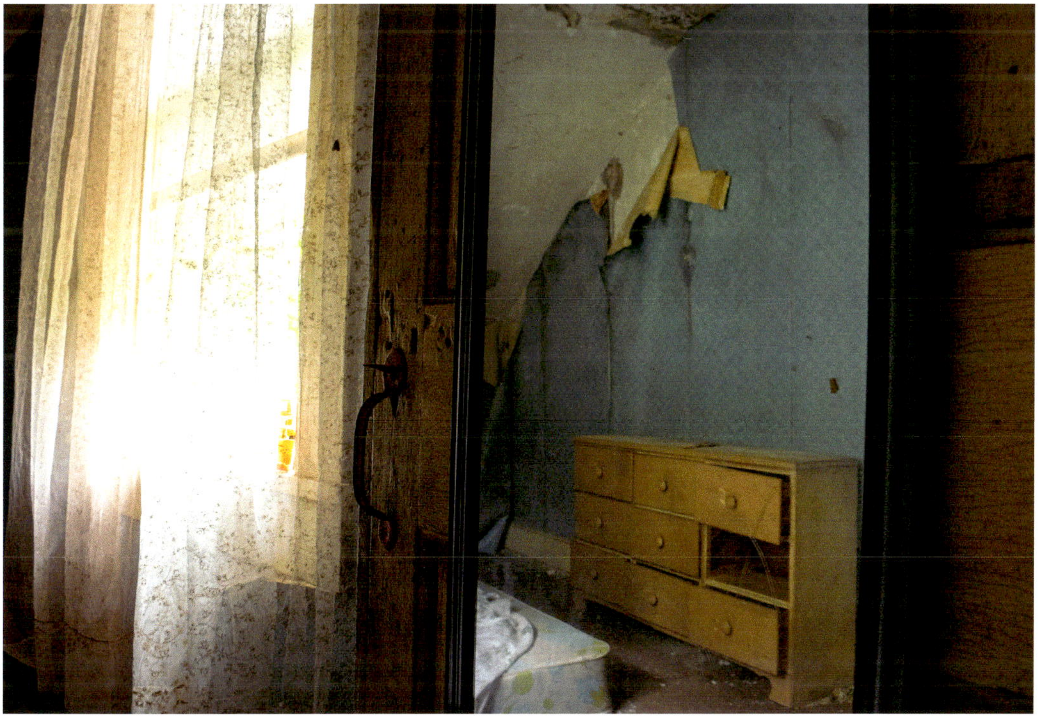

Reflecting upon decay—a closet door mirror shows a chest of drawers and sagging blue wallpaper in reverse.

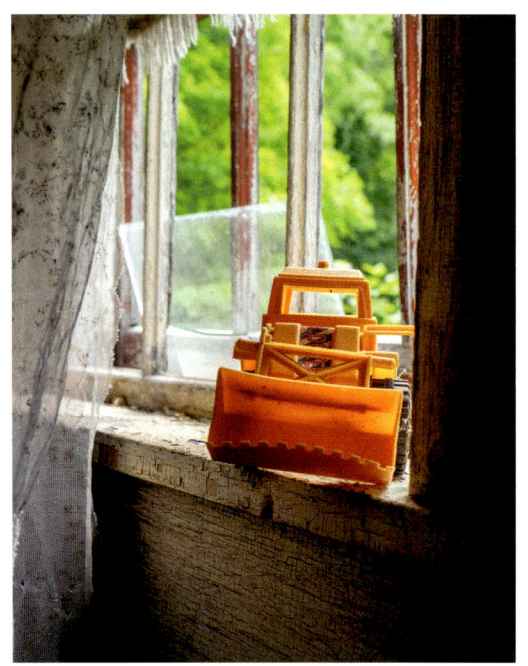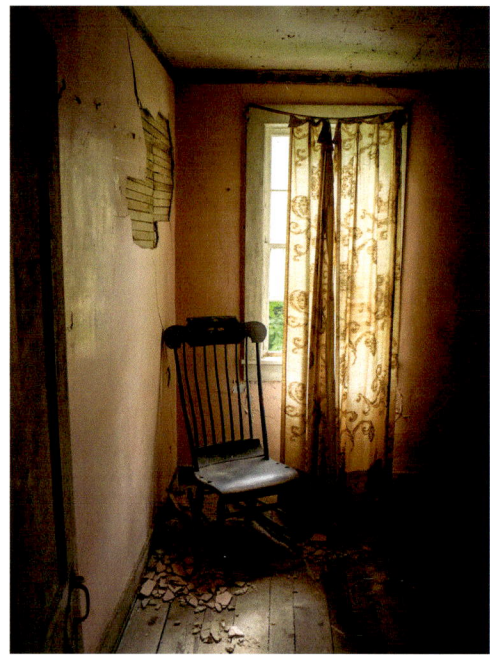

Above left: An unexpected toy found perched on a windowsill behind sheer curtains.

Above right: Another black rocking chair invites explorers to take a rest. Antique door hardware in the foreground is a reminder of the many original features within this eighteenth-century cape.

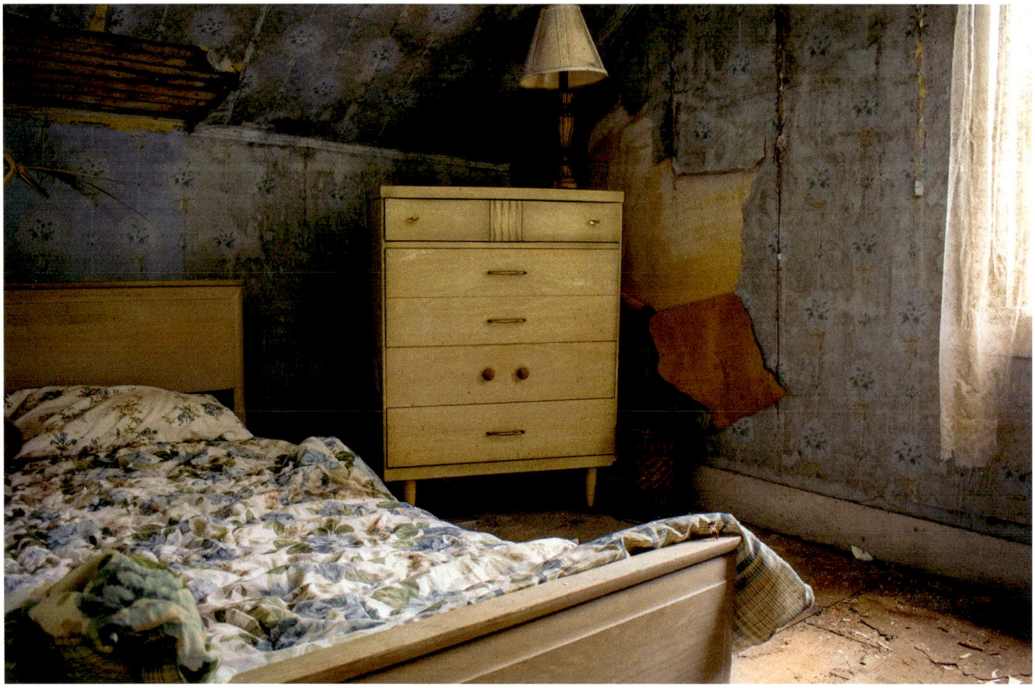

Someone has bothered to arrange this furniture from *Dead Souls* into a new configuration. The waste basket in the corner remains empty.

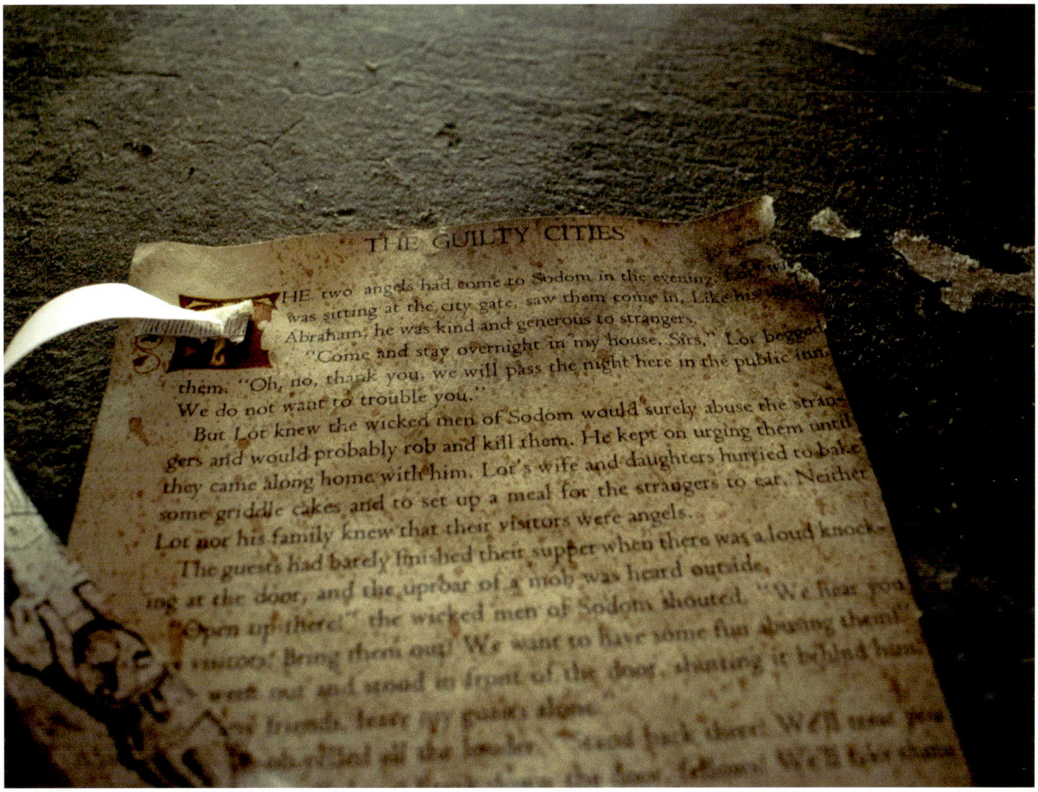

THE GUILTY CITIES

THE two angels had come to Sodom in the evening, ... was sitting at the city gate, saw them come in. Like his ... Abraham, he was kind and generous to strangers.

"Come and stay overnight in my house, Sirs," Lot begged them. "Oh, no, thank you, we will pass the night here in the public inn. We do not want to trouble you."

But Lot knew the wicked men of Sodom would surely abuse the strangers and would probably rob and kill them. He kept on urging them until they came along home with him. Lot's wife and daughters hurried to bake some griddle cakes and to set up a meal for the strangers to eat. Neither Lot nor his family knew that their visitors were angels.

The guests had barely finished their supper when there was a loud knocking at the door, and the uproar of a mob was heard outside.

"Open up there!" the wicked men of Sodom shouted. "We hear you ... visitors! Bring them out! We want to have some fun abusing them!" ... went out and stood in front of the door, shutting it behind him. ...

A page from a religious text lies on an upstairs table; this movie prop belonged to the story's father, a wayward preacher on a quest for immortality.

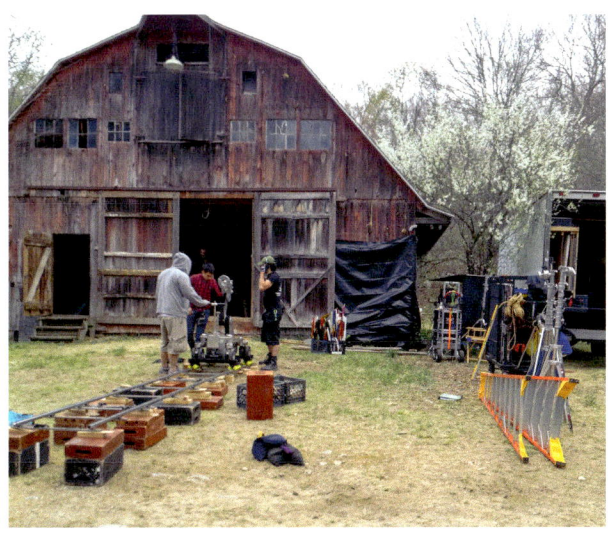

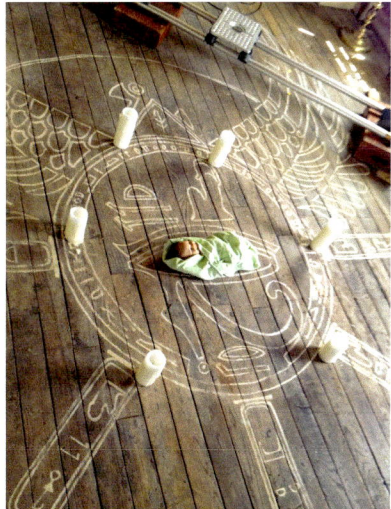

Above left: The crew readies a tracking shot for a scene outside the film's evocative barn. (*Photo courtesy of Colin Theys*)

Above right: Setting up to shoot one of the movie's occult ceremonies using a baby doll stand-in. (*Photo courtesy of Colin Theys*)

2

THE CRUMBLING MILL

T his sprawling mill complex was partially destroyed by fire years ago, leaving what remains to continue its slow decay alongside a railroad track that runs through the center of a small town. At one time the most important location in this community, fate has left it an eyesore that many residents only wish to forget. Today, the worst of the destruction is hidden by trees and brush, making it barely visible from a children's playground just a few feet away.

Visiting the site provides a lesson on the many ways in which buildings can fall apart. Bringing to mind post-war ruins, some look as if flattened by bomb blasts, their original appearance mostly left to the imagination. Others are hollowed-out shells, roofs crumpled within their red brick walls as though shaken to the ground by an earthquake. Nevertheless, architectural interest can still be found around every corner, even if it comes in bits and pieces. From beautifully designed facades to the odds and ends of the mill's antique construction, remnants of its former glory peek out from the shadows like pieces of a giant, disassembled Lego set. And, notably, a few examples of large machinery are left standing amid the rubble as if rising from the ashes, ready for a final shift that will never come. Bearing venerable names such as Lombard and Lake Eerie Engineering Corp., these heavy hydraulic presses were used in the manufacturing of office furniture by one of the last businesses housed here.

Structures that have not yet fully collapsed reveal environments largely stripped of furnishings and equipment. Even so, the interiors feel chaotic with piles of debris and peeling paint—hardly empty. And there are other signs of a human presence beyond the prolific graffiti and vandalism. Stools, buckets, and random tools float upon a sea of detritus that litters the landscape. A surviving second-floor office features a large, moldy recliner and a topless desk that looks like it could fall through the floor at any moment. In a basement, a sign for "money orders" outside a crumbling chamber serves as a reminder that these rooms were used by hardworking people with very specific jobs.

Built *c.* 1906 to produce fine cotton goods, the facility once employed up to 1,200 workers, many of whom lived in nearby company housing. Wage disputes during the mid-1930s prompted a labor strike and eventual selloff and liquidation of its inventory, after which various companies took a turn at renting out the premises. These included makers of robes, storage cabinets, and even a recycling operation until the complex finally fell into abandonment around 1995.

Derelict factories of this scale represent an enormous, and expensive, challenge for local governments to grapple with. From the remediation of toxic materials to the multimillion-dollar price tag of demolishing and clearing the properties, state and federal funding is often required before any redevelopment is possible—even as decades pass with little or no "progress." This particular mill has seen significant efforts before, mostly aimed at addressing the immediate dangers to the community while leaving much of the ruins intact. Still, change comes in waves: In 2024, Connecticut announced more than $26 million in grants to address blighted properties across the state, including in Eastern Connecticut, geared toward preparing the sites for new uses. In the meantime, documenting and appreciating these relics before they are gone remains its own priority, with the window to do so closing one day, and disaster, at a time.

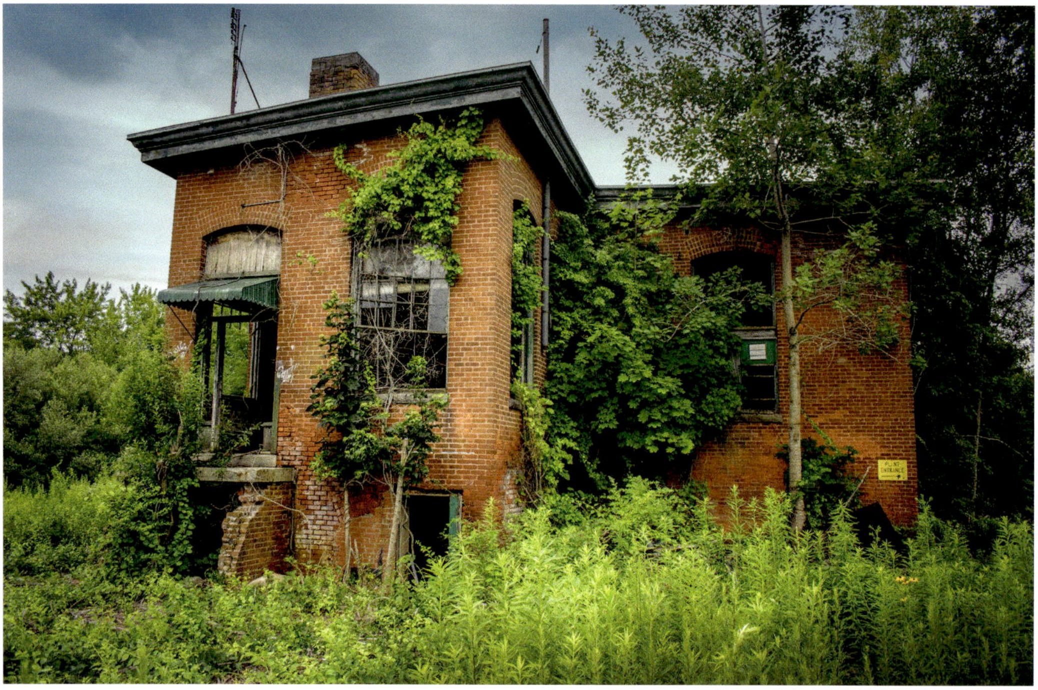

One of the remaining mill buildings appears to have served as an office. A small green awning covered steps that have since been demolished.

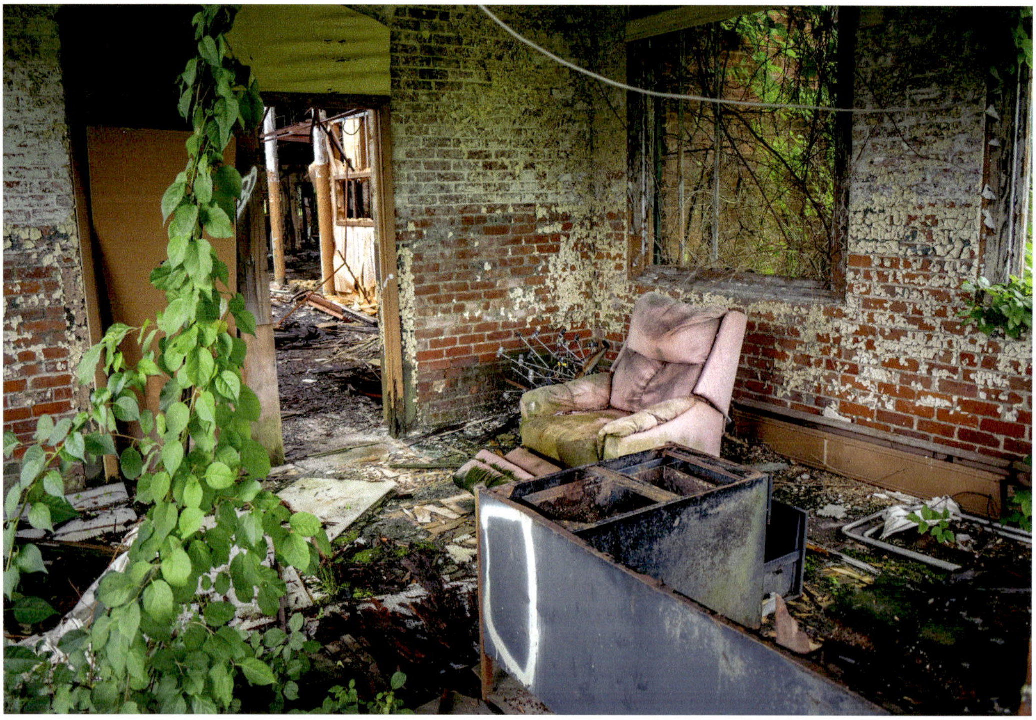

Up the missing stairs, a vestibule with scattered furniture is slowly invaded by vines through its many broken windows.

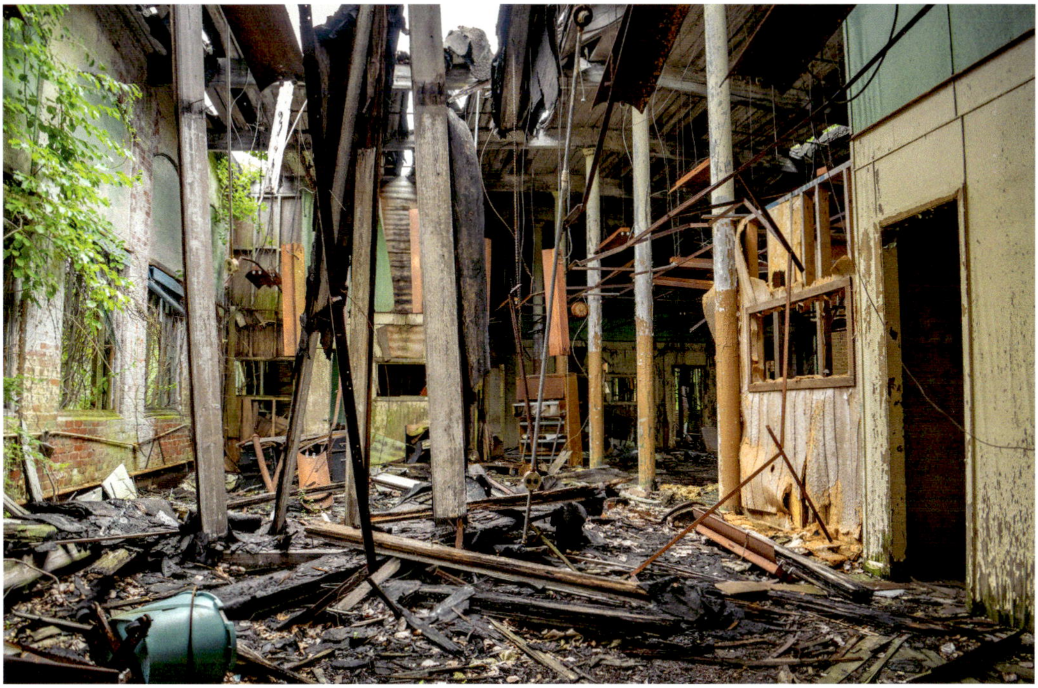

The main floor of the office space has begun to collapse in several places. In the distance, a tall storage cabinet holds oversized documents.

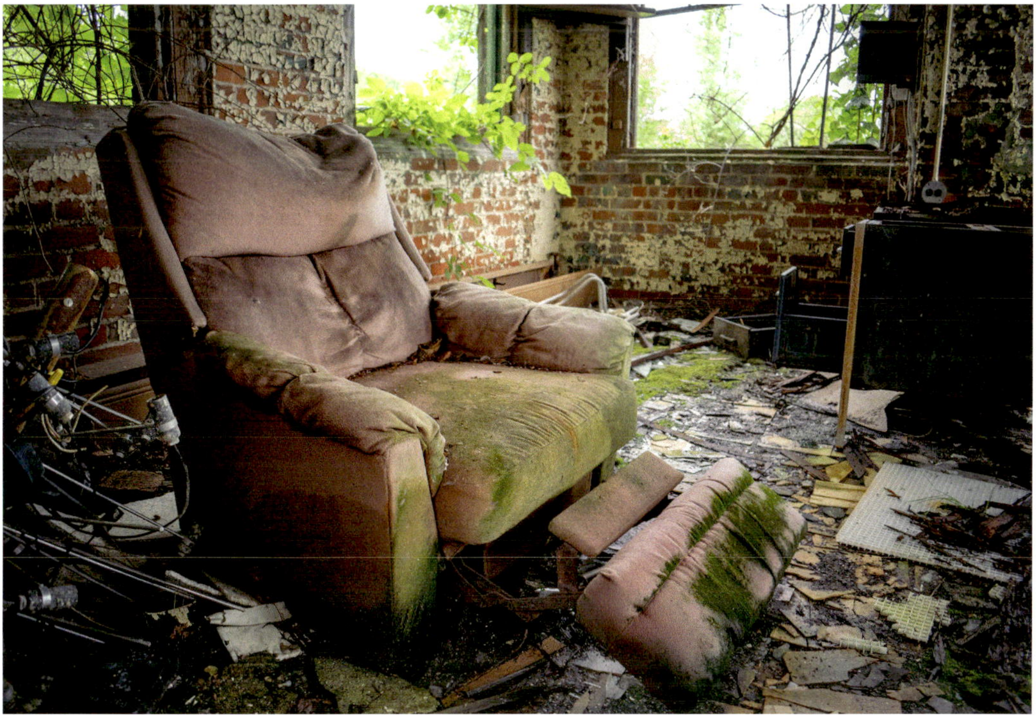

This plush, pink recliner is not as inviting as it used to be.

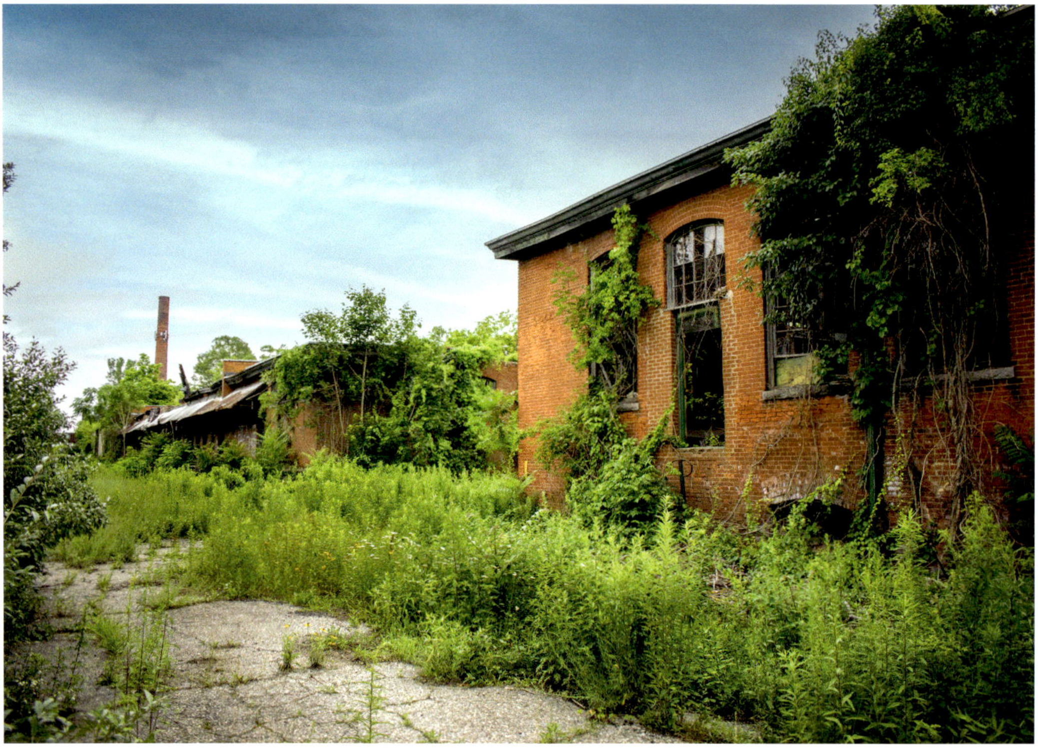

A row of mill ruins, their facades facing a paved area that has become almost invisible beneath overgrowth.

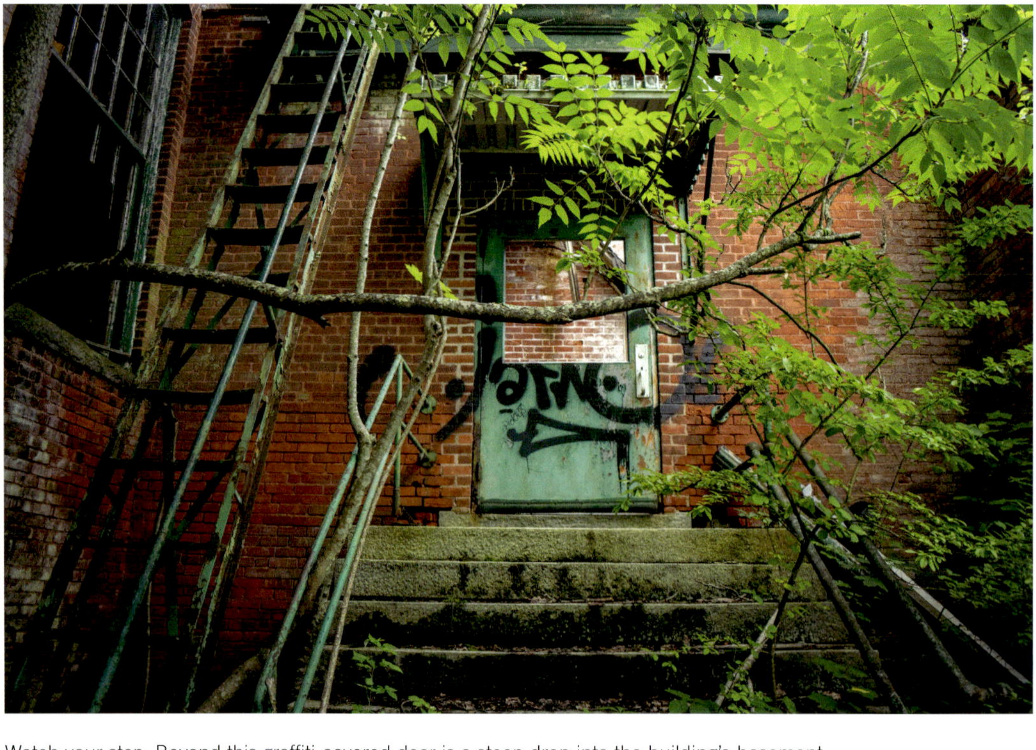

Watch your step. Beyond this graffiti-covered door is a steep drop into the building's basement.

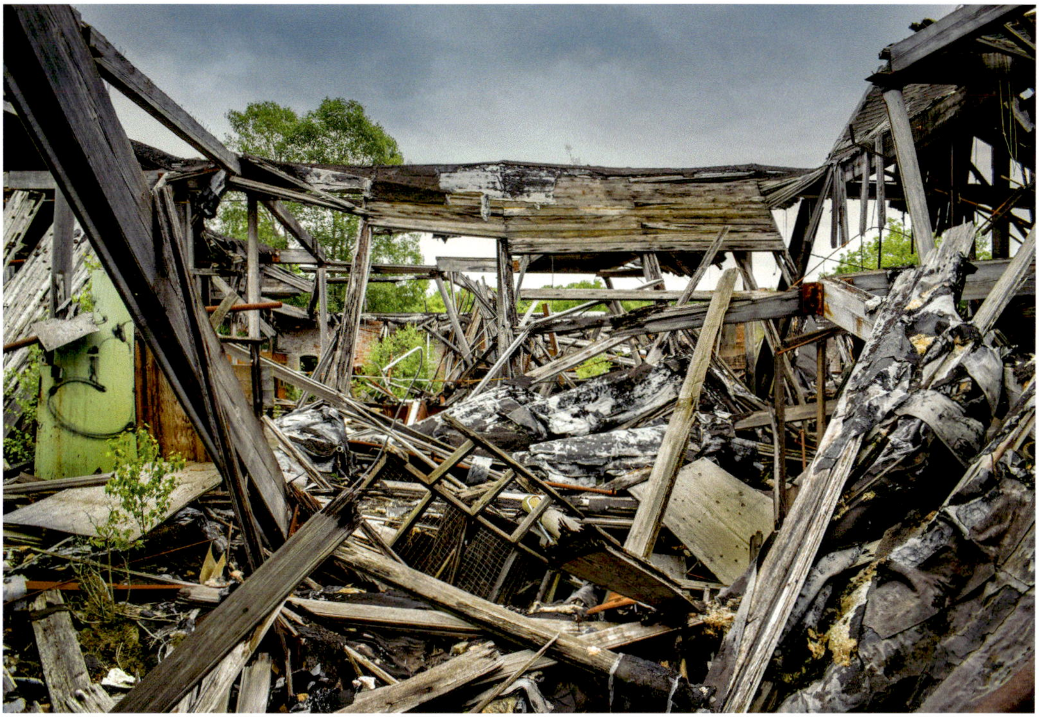

Much of the site consists of a huge debris field. Piles of materials with no discernable form make this part of the mill look as though destroyed by aerial bombardment.

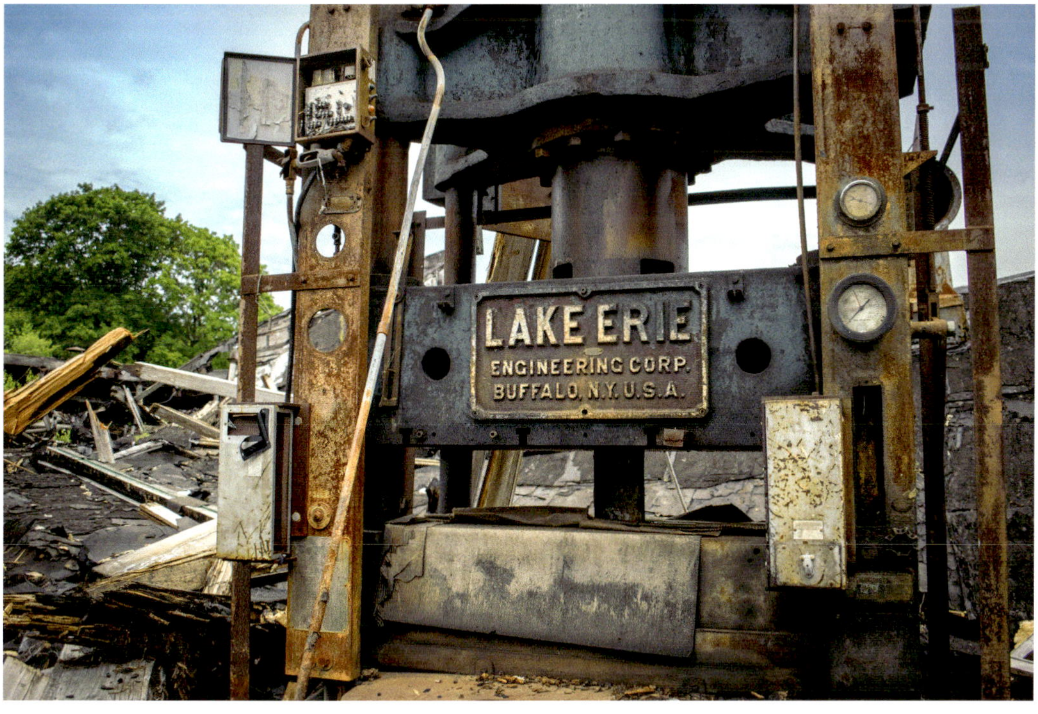

The venerable Lake Erie Engineering Corporation produced a wide range of hydraulic machinery such as this mid-century metal forming press.

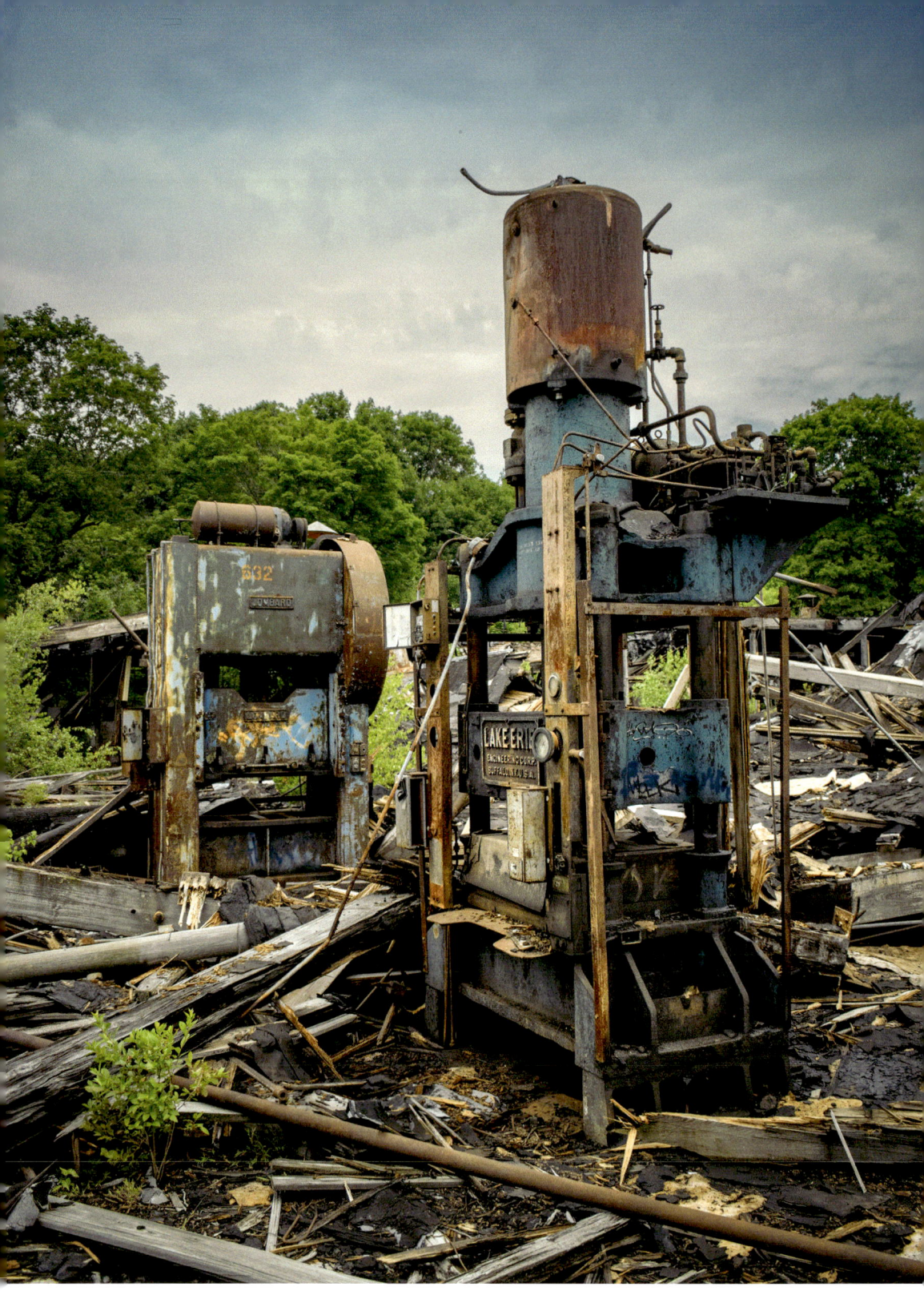

A pair of industrial presses rise heroically from the rubble. These machines had been covered by a semblance of a roof only six months earlier.

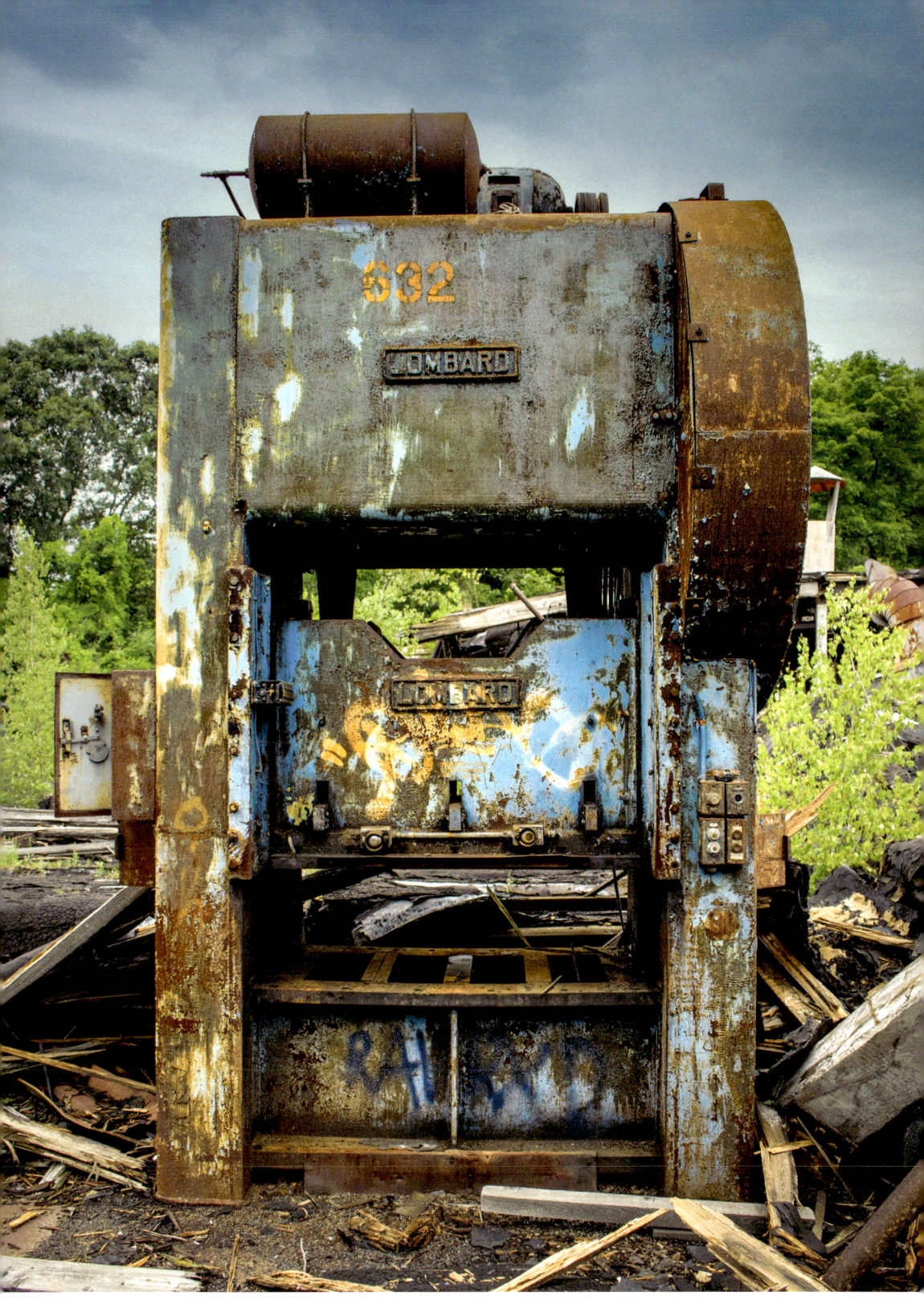

This heavy extrusion press was used by a manufacturer of office furniture, one of the last companies to operate in the mill.

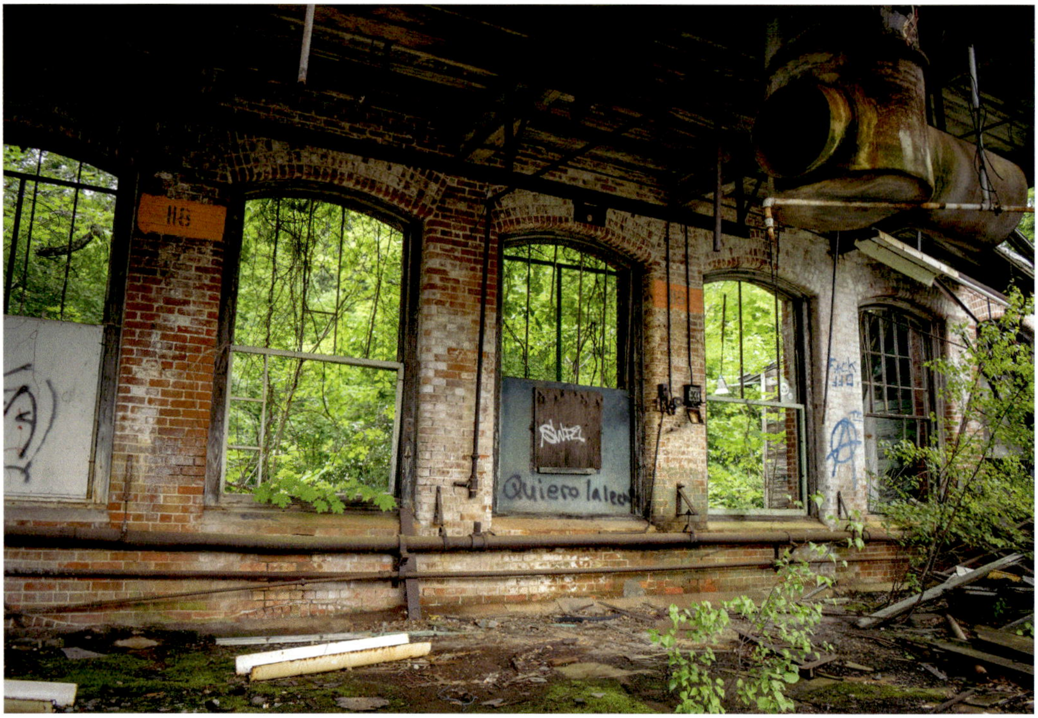

A wall of beautiful arched windows is nearly all that remains of this structure.

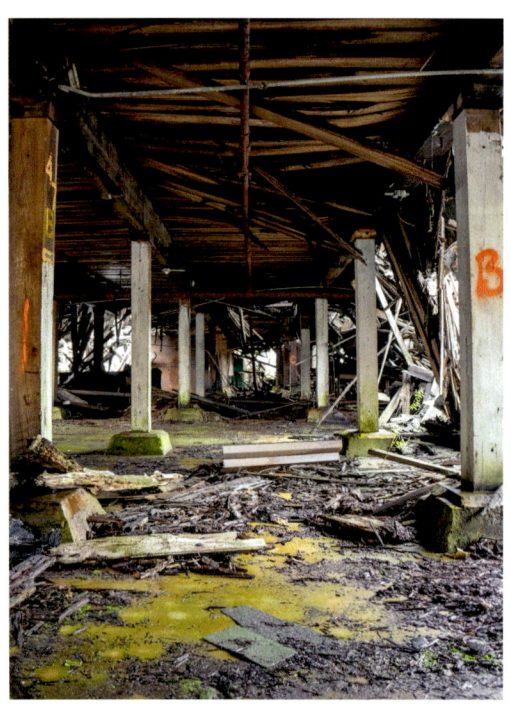

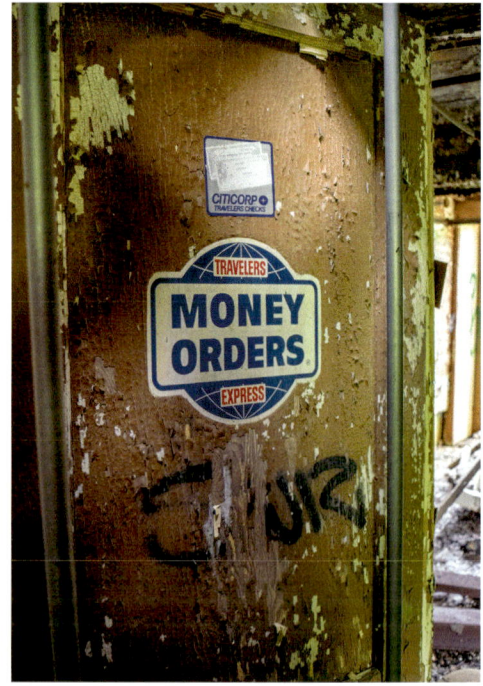

Above left: Large wooden columns still bear the weight of a rotting floor above.

Above right: If you are searching here for money orders or traveler's checks, you will need a time machine.

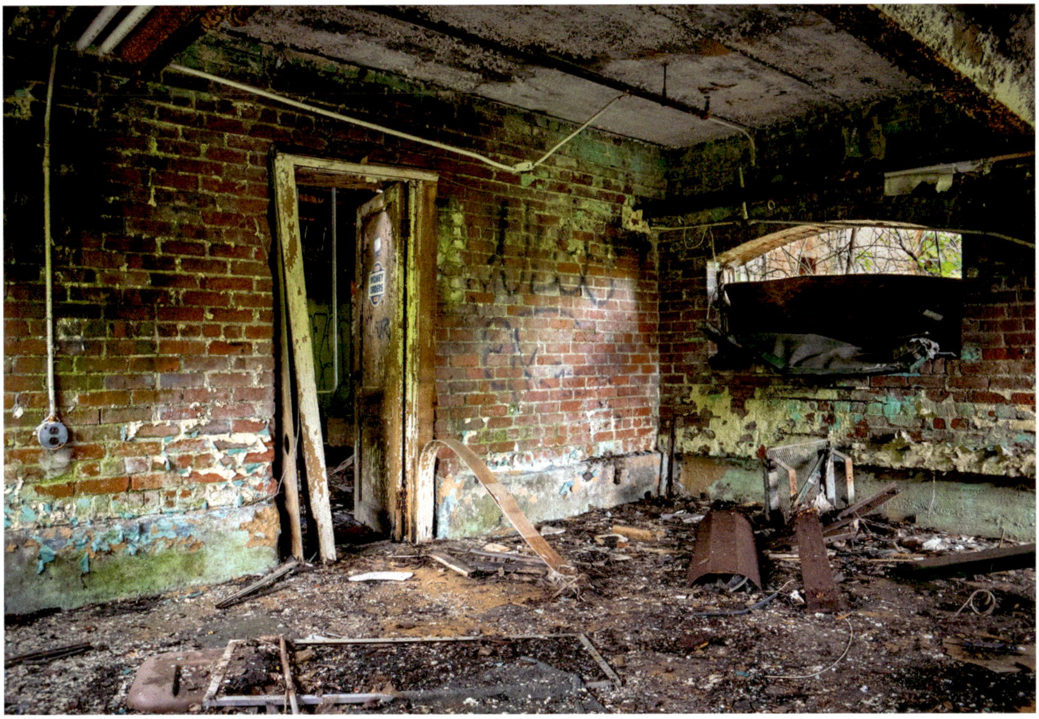

Just enough paint is left to determine that this room was once a very bright blue.

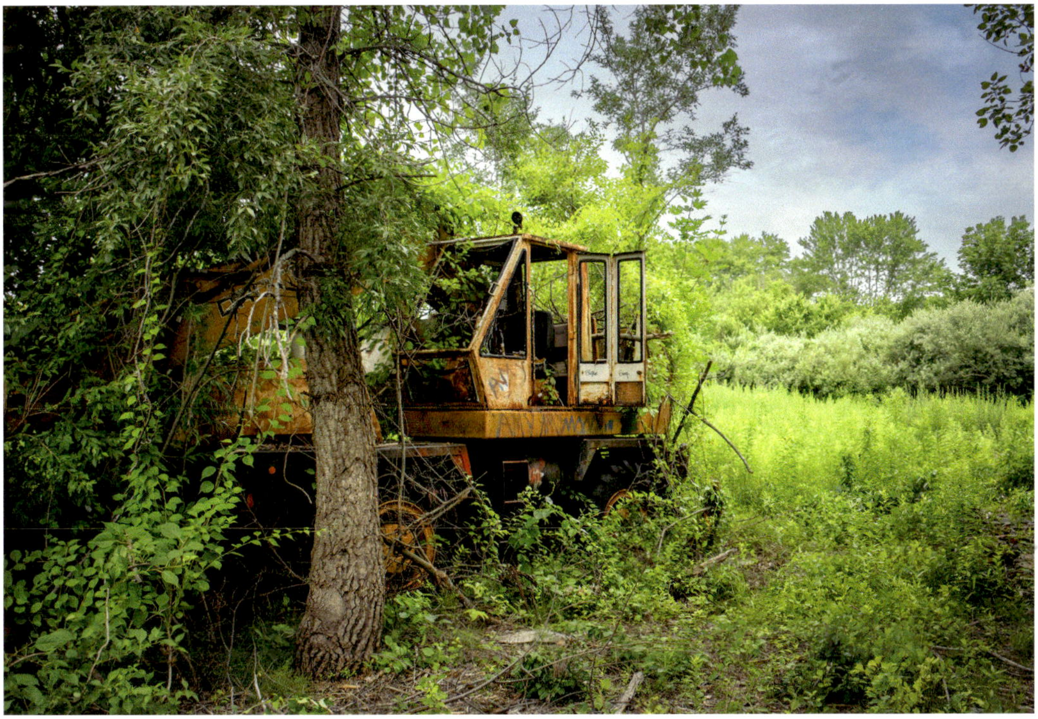

A lonely excavator bears witness to abandoned cleanup efforts.

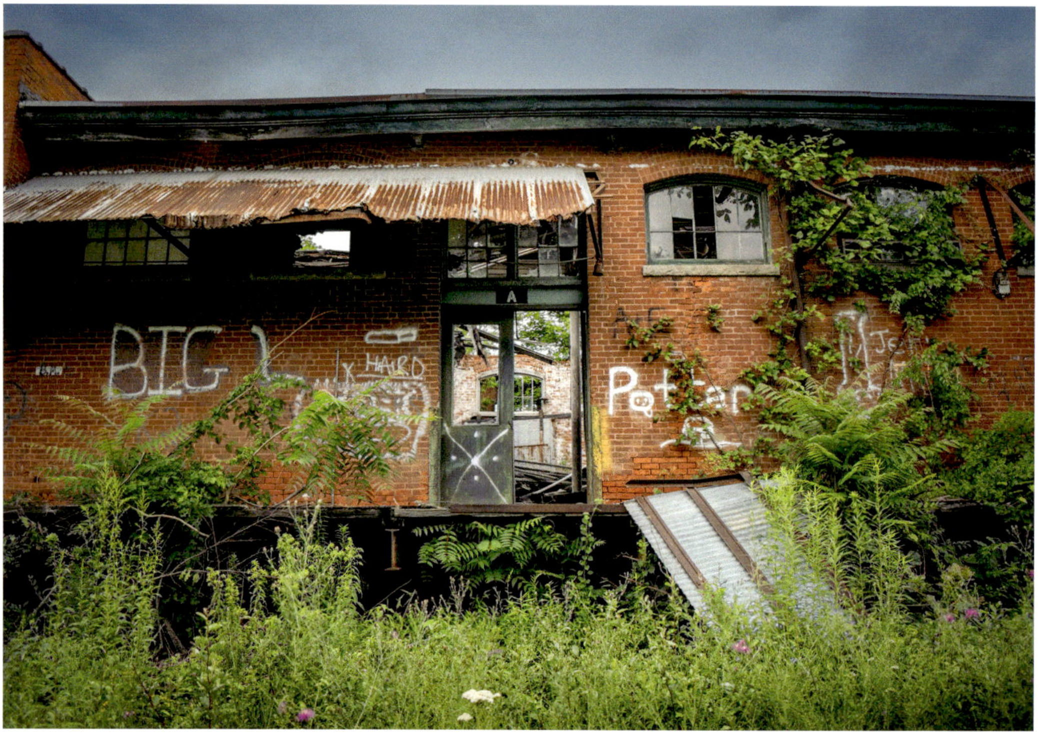

The architecture of this old building can still be appreciated despite its missing roof.

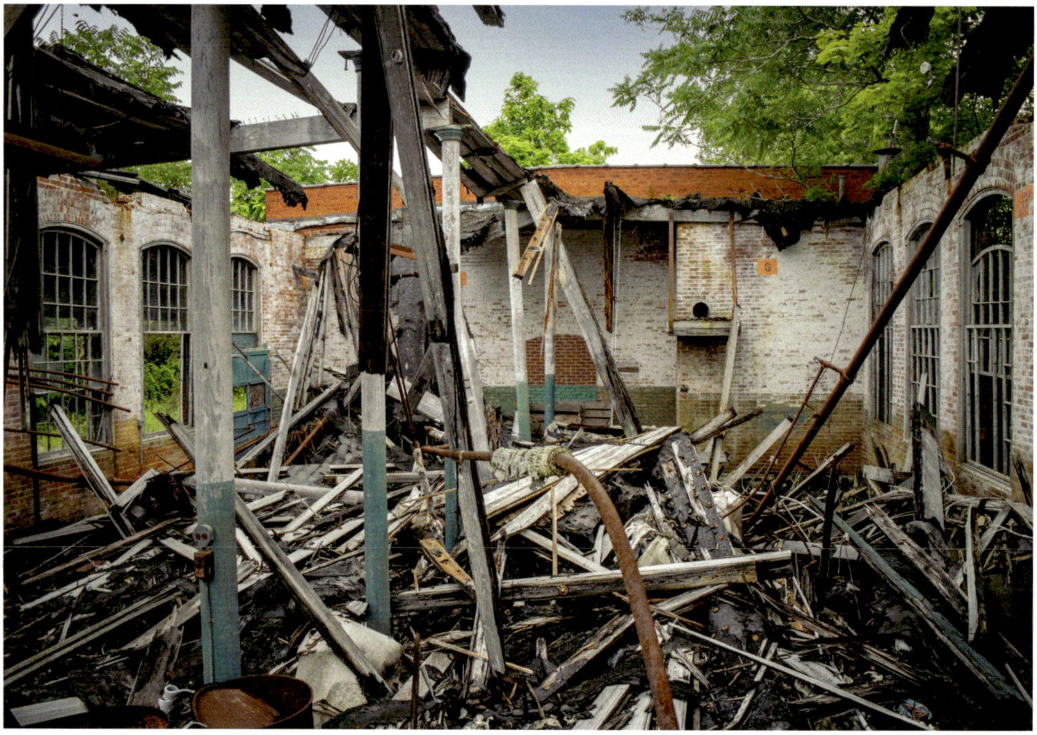

Inside the roofless building, with remnants of a turquoise and white paint scheme.

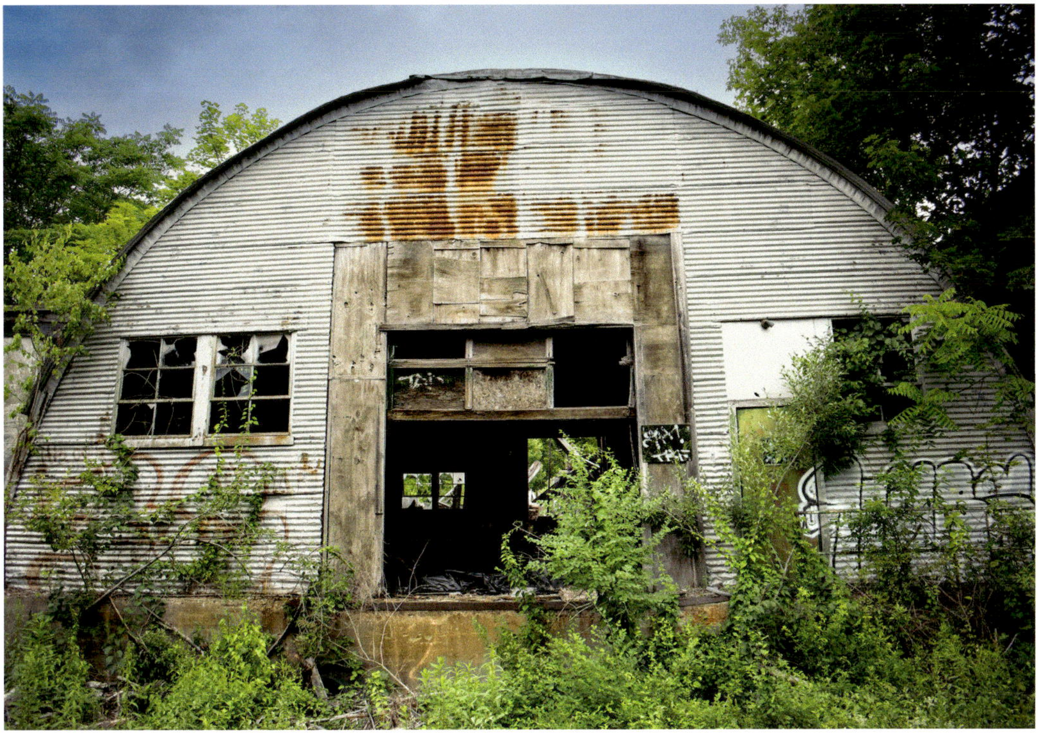

This Quonset hut has held up surprisingly well compared to the rest of the site.

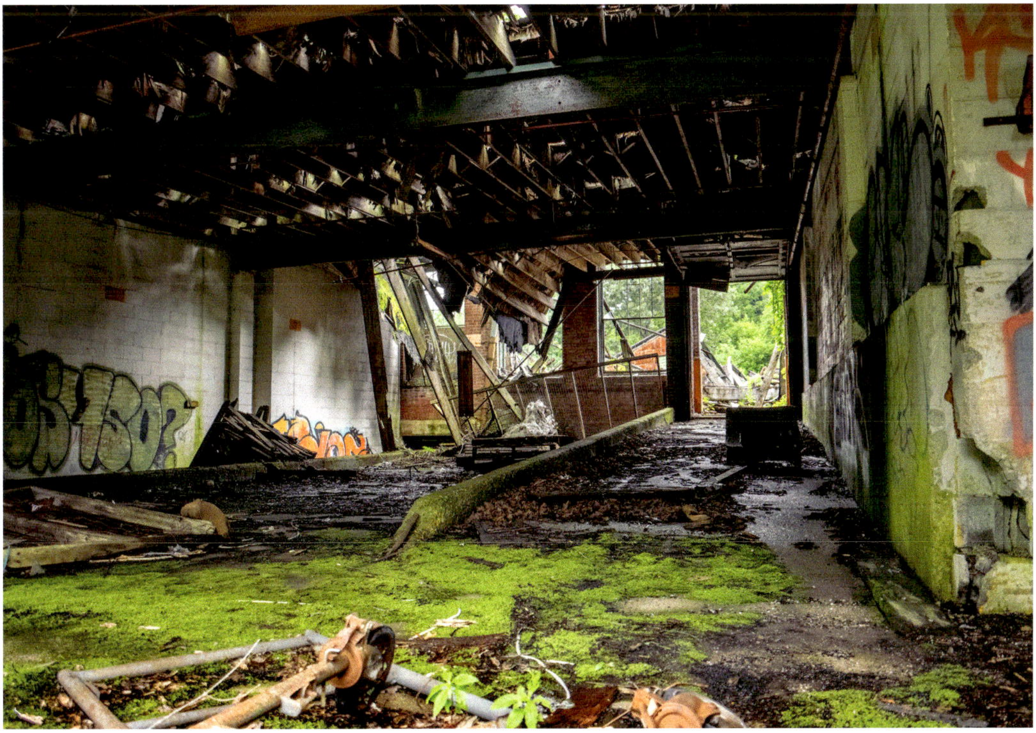

A drab shipping area has been brightened up by moss and graffiti.

3

THE DERELICT DAIRY

From a distance, the buildings here look like an overgrown shipwreck. Covered in a thick blanket of vines, most structures have succumbed to an oppressive mixture of water damage and plant weight. What is left deteriorates by the day as nature reclaims it at a slow yet inexorable pace. This abandoned place, once clear of debris and full of the sounds of cattle and farm life, contributed to New England's vibrant dairy industry for many years.

Dating as far back as the 1600s, dairy farming has been a staple of Connecticut agriculture from the time of the first European settlers. By the 1950s, technological advances in milk production saw the state become a leader in innovation, with numerous operations turning exclusively to this profitable business. However, as long-distance milk transport became more viable, the competition from faraway parts of the country began to erode local suppliers. Suffering from higher regional costs to bring their products to market, a majority were forced to close down.

Shifting consumer preferences also took their toll—with the rise of heart-healthy diets in the 1970s, whole milk was targeted as beverage non grata. Americans began to drink and eat less dairy in general as trendy alternatives arrived at the grocery store. Today, there are less than 10 percent of the number of dairy farms nationwide that existed a half century ago. As iconic as a glass of New England milk might be, it is simply not the mainstay it once was.

Nevertheless, Eastern Connecticut is still home to tireless farmers who have succeeded despite the economic challenges, contributing to a valuable sector of the state's agricultural output that accounts for thousands of jobs and over 400 million pounds of milk annually. Their offerings, especially popular among those who prefer to buy local, can be readily found in area grocery stores where they are still sold in traditional glass bottles meant to be returned after each use (assuming you want your hefty deposit back).

Exploring these derelict buildings across several seasons reveals how fast even robust mid-century structures can fail when left unattended. The pole barn, which seems to show further collapse on each visit, appears to have accommodated around fifty cows, marking it as a fairly small example. An attached milking room is in even worse shape, although its vintage DeLaval brand equipment remains largely intact. The herringbone configuration of the space, now a crumbling mess, allowed up to eight animals to be positioned at an angle for easier maneuvering and access from the milker's pit below. Outside, a quaint illustration of a spotted cow faces the roadside, the only identifying remnant of a site long submerged in overgrowth. While the eventual fate of this 80-acre property might have included unsightly redevelopment, its sale to the state in 2001 has ensured that both its legacy and beauty will survive.

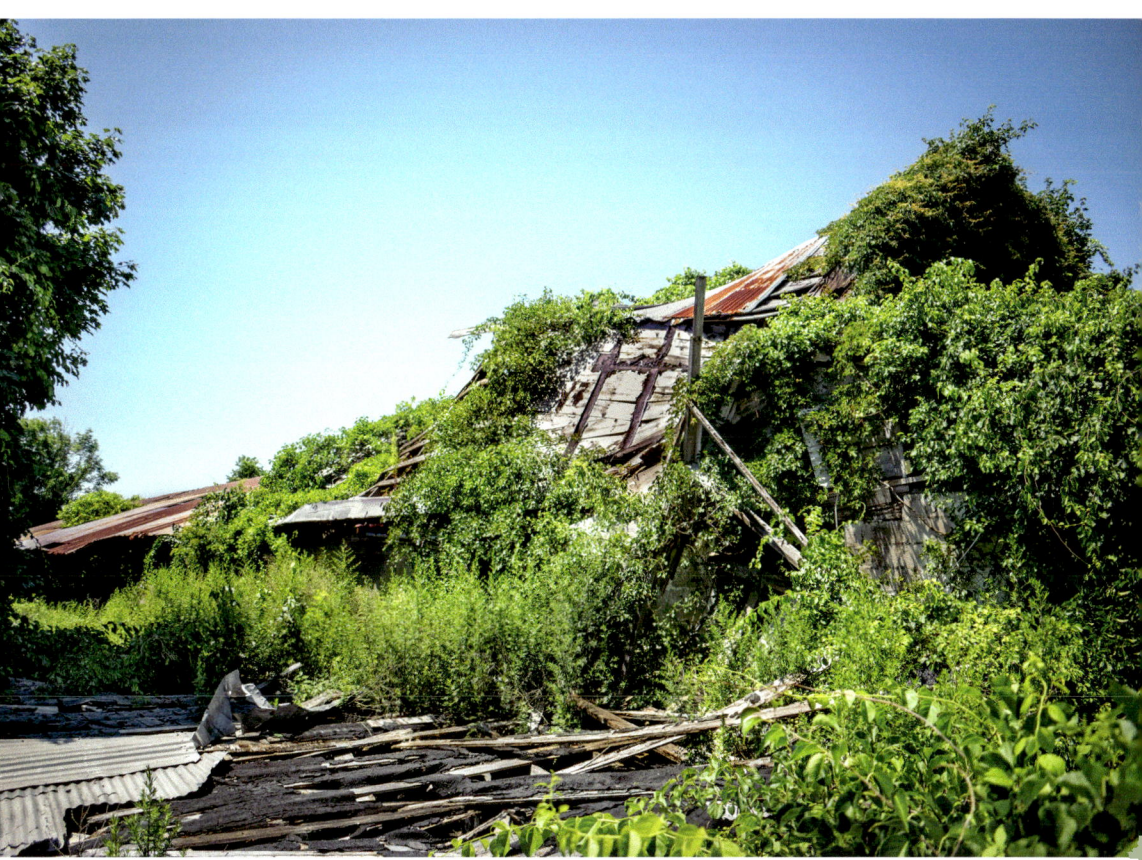

From a distance, the farm buildings resemble an overgrown shipwreck.

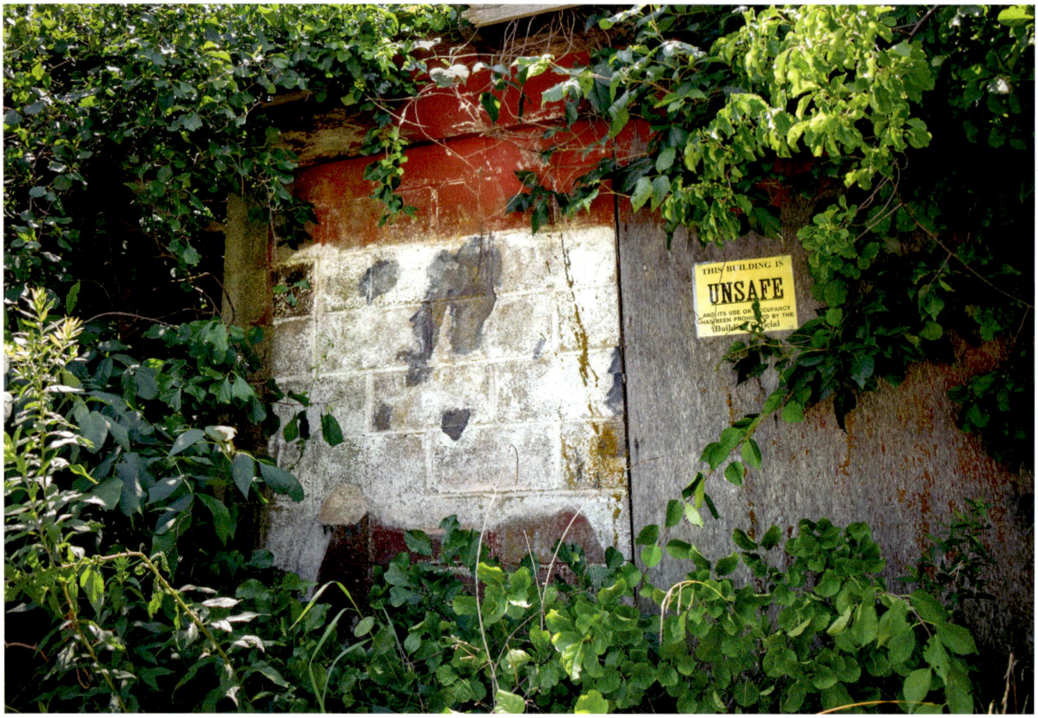

A quaint illustration of a spotted dairy cow faces the roadside, the only remaining sign of what was produced here.

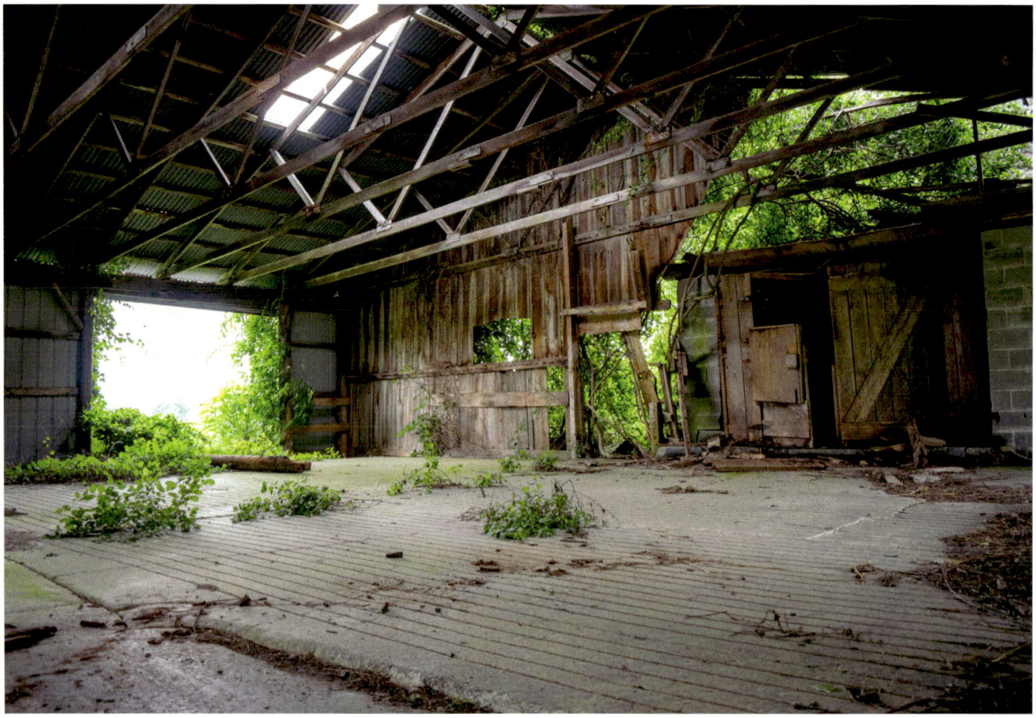

The interior of this large pole barn has seen better days.

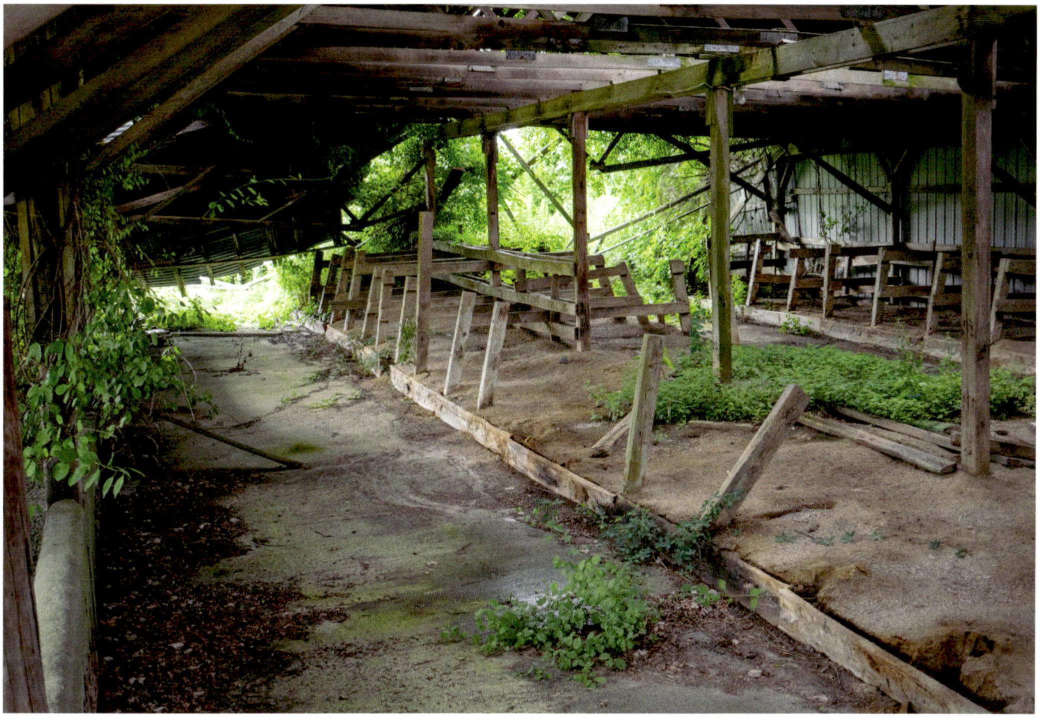

Freestall pen layouts include a space for each cow to feed and lie down. This example appears to have housed fifty to sixty animals.

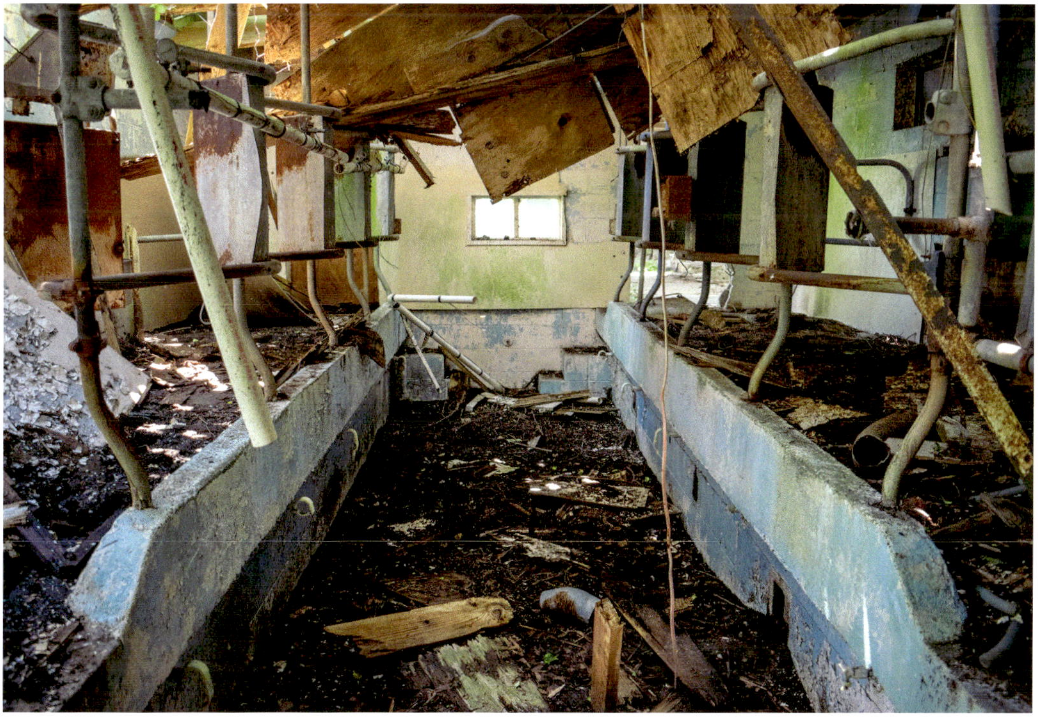

A view of the milker's pit with a collapsing ceiling. It has been many years since anyone used this space.

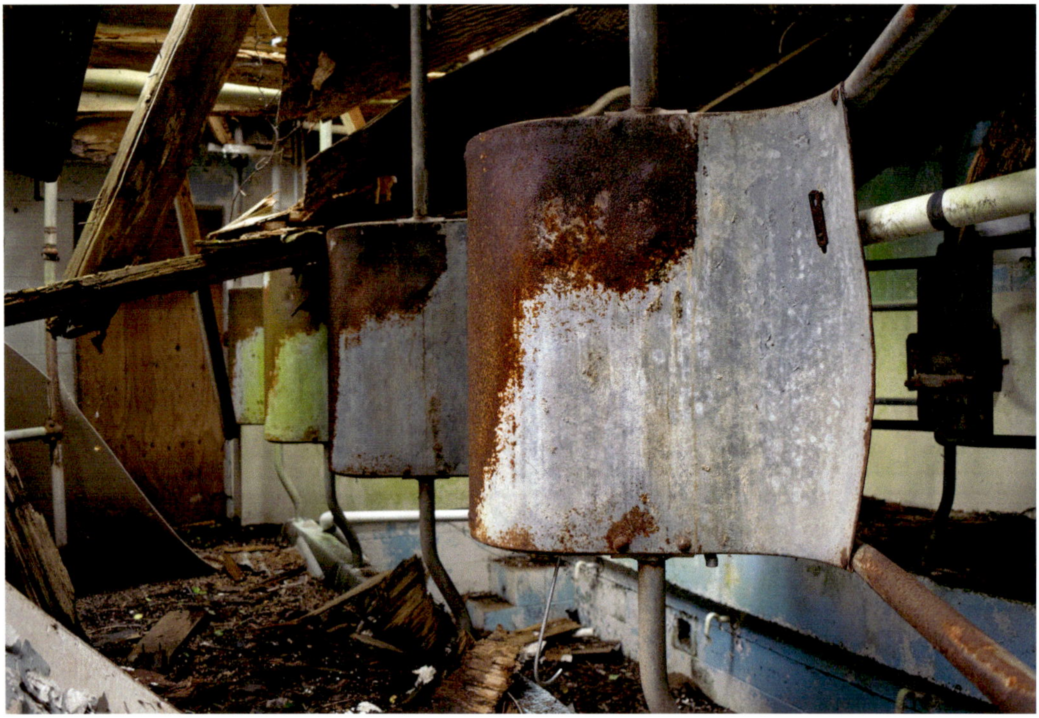

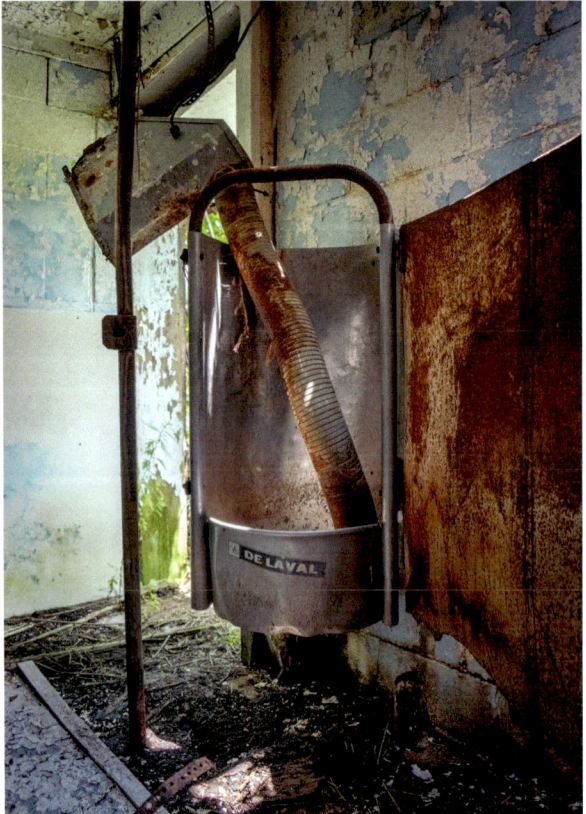

Above: This milking room's herringbone configuration allowed for cows to be positioned at an efficient angle.

Left: Vintage cattle feeders line the walls where cows were milked.

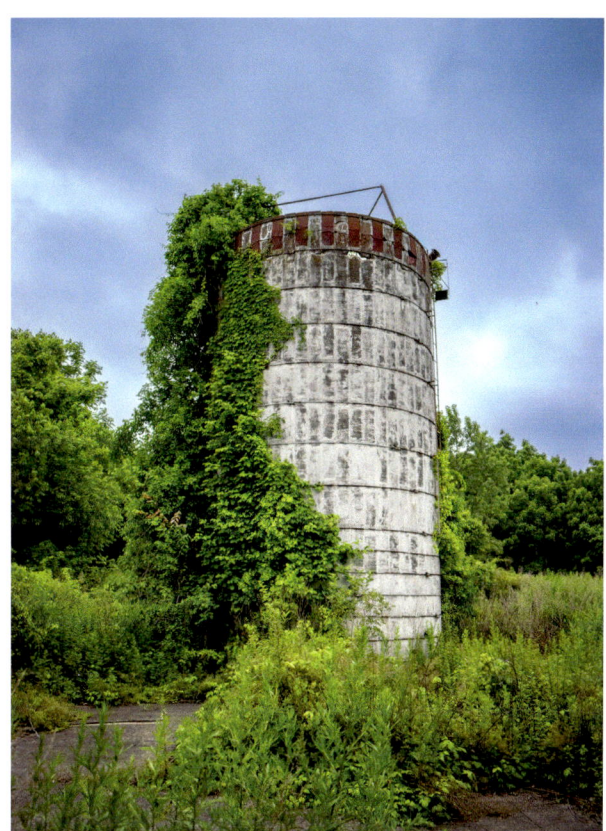

Right: An old steel tower silo once stored feed for the herd.

Below: The derelict farm still contributes to a picturesque rural scene.

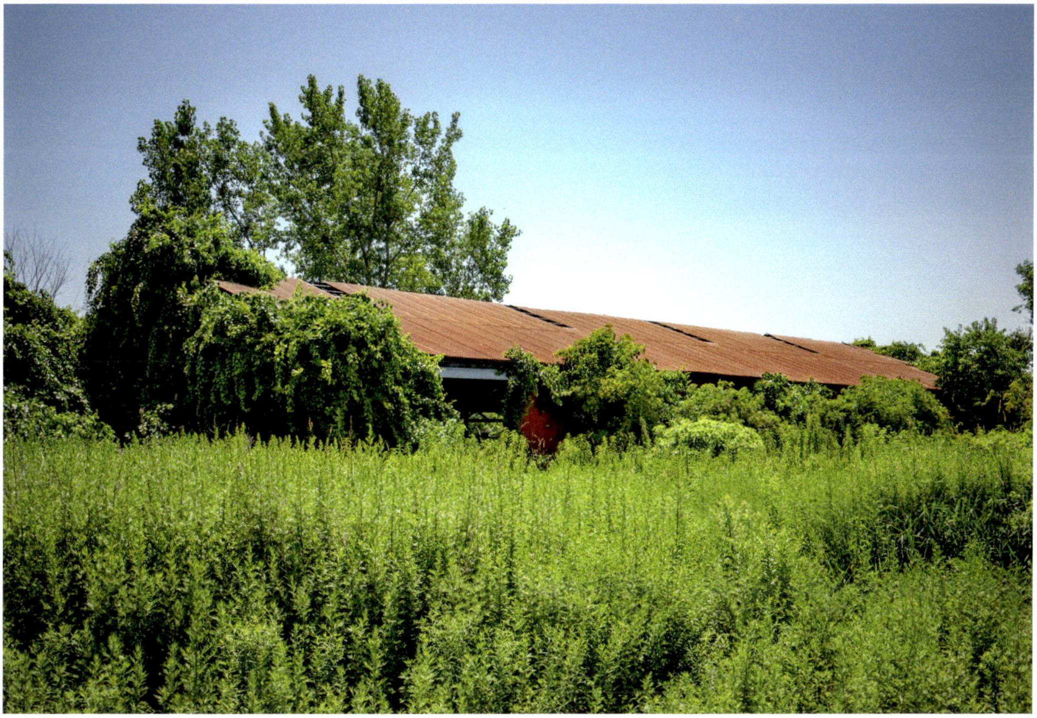

4

THE COUNTRY GHOST

They say that only three things can kill an old house: fire, water, and bugs. While the speed and drama of a house fire might bring local news coverage, and stubborn insects pose a perennial threat to wooden posts and beams, water damage often yields a quieter and more preventable death that arrives, quite literally, in a slow drip. As recently as ten years ago, this Victorian-era farmhouse appeared intact, with no visible signs of damage to the exterior. However, a minor sag on one side of the roof—the eventual epicenter of decay—foretold a disaster that has now brought this relic to the point of no return, an unfortunate victim of extreme neglect.

Although antique homes have a reputation as being drafty and perhaps expensive to own, they are overbuilt by today's standards, possessing a degree of quality and attention to detail that remains timeless. Modern materials may allow for speedy construction and architectural feats that couldn't be achieved in the past, but their mass-produced nature renders them inherently disposable. In contrast, a great deal of New England's period buildings are handmade treasures that cannot be replaced—the work of skilled craftsmen who spent a lifetime mastering techniques that enable their creations to stand proudly for centuries. But once they are gone, they are gone forever, and, sadly, each year their numbers dwindle. Some burn, some are dismantled to make way for new development, and others, like the example in this chapter, suffer the cascading effects of a small leak that eventually leads to a shocking demise—leaving behind another ghost on the landscape.

Dating to 1840, this center-hall beauty sits on 100 pristine acres, with bucolic views of pastures, a winding brook, and even a lovely pond to complete its perfect country setting. While the property's current state of collapse appears to have come on relatively quickly, the lack of furnishings or signs of habitation within the house indicates it has likely been abandoned for much longer. The back of the home is the only traversable portion, being farthest from the destruction that has already brought down entire rooms in the front, where missing floors and exposed walls inadvertently reveal the building's inner structure.

Still, some hints of a past life are scattered about. Upstairs, a large bed huddles in the corner as if trying to stay clear of a growing hole on the other side of the chamber. On a wooden dresser with a large mirror that reflects the afternoon sunlight, a single glass bowl provides a vivid splash of green to break the brown-and-white monotony. A worse-for-wear 1920s tabletop phonograph, found outside the upstairs hallway, is one of the only personal objects left behind. No doubt, it contributed to many an evening's entertainment in this classic New England home. Now, it seems the old hand-cranked record player was destined to serve as just a bittersweet reminder of better days.

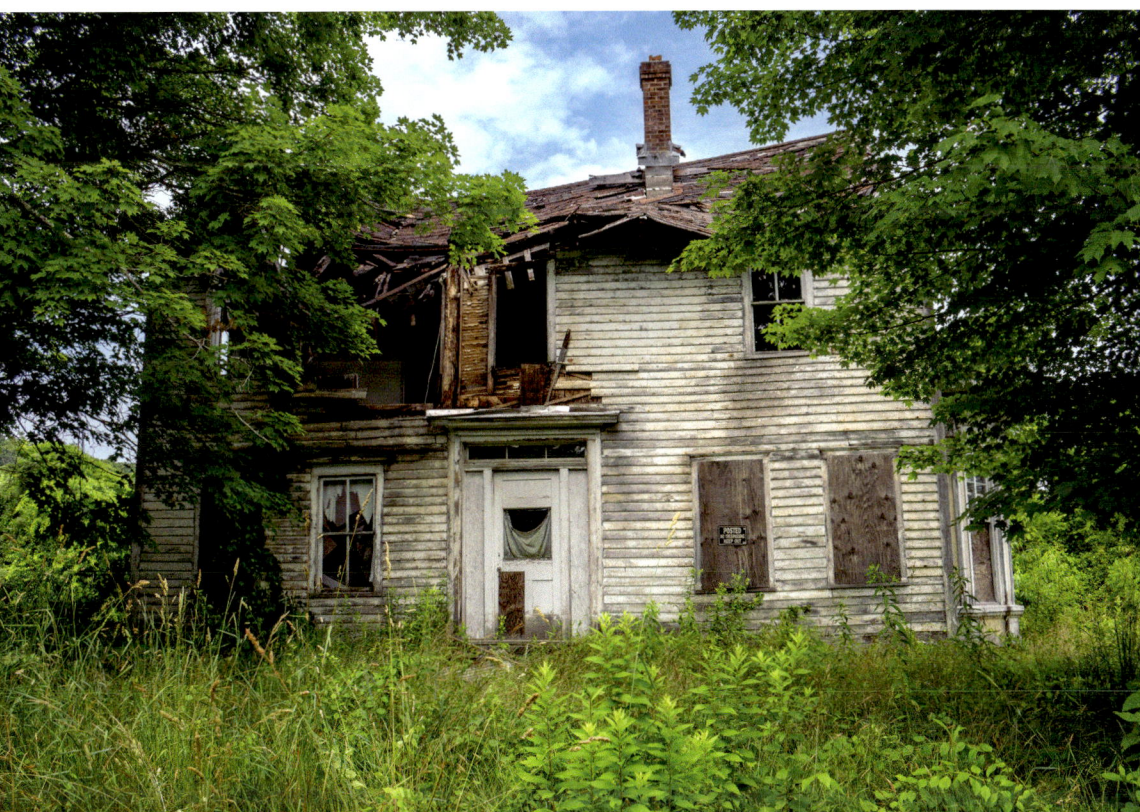

Incredibly, the house's roof and façade were fully intact less than ten years ago, reflecting the rapid deterioration water can bring to even overbuilt structures.

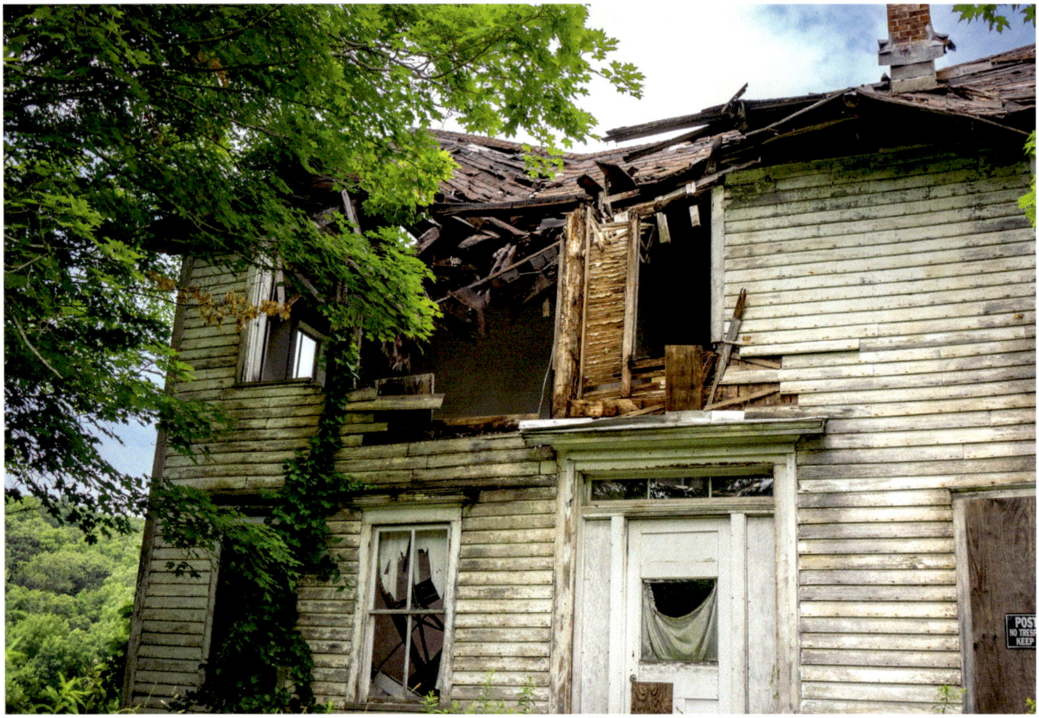

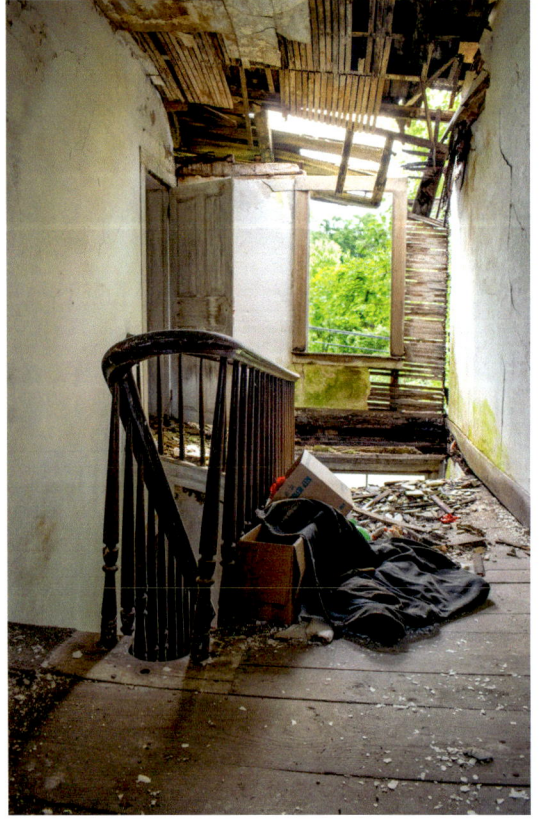

Above: Looking closer at the damage offers a view of period materials and construction that were never meant to be seen.

Left: The home's central hallway is now open to the elements, exposing antique lath from the plaster walls and ceiling.

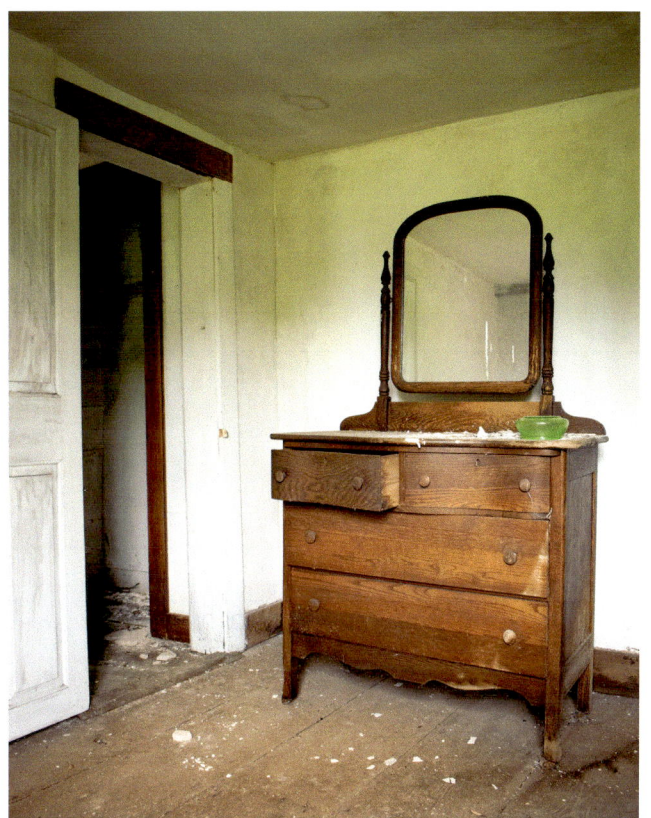

Right: One of the house's few remaining items of furniture is illuminated by afternoon sunlight.

Below: A glass bowl atop an old dresser provides a splash of color to break the brown-and-white monotony.

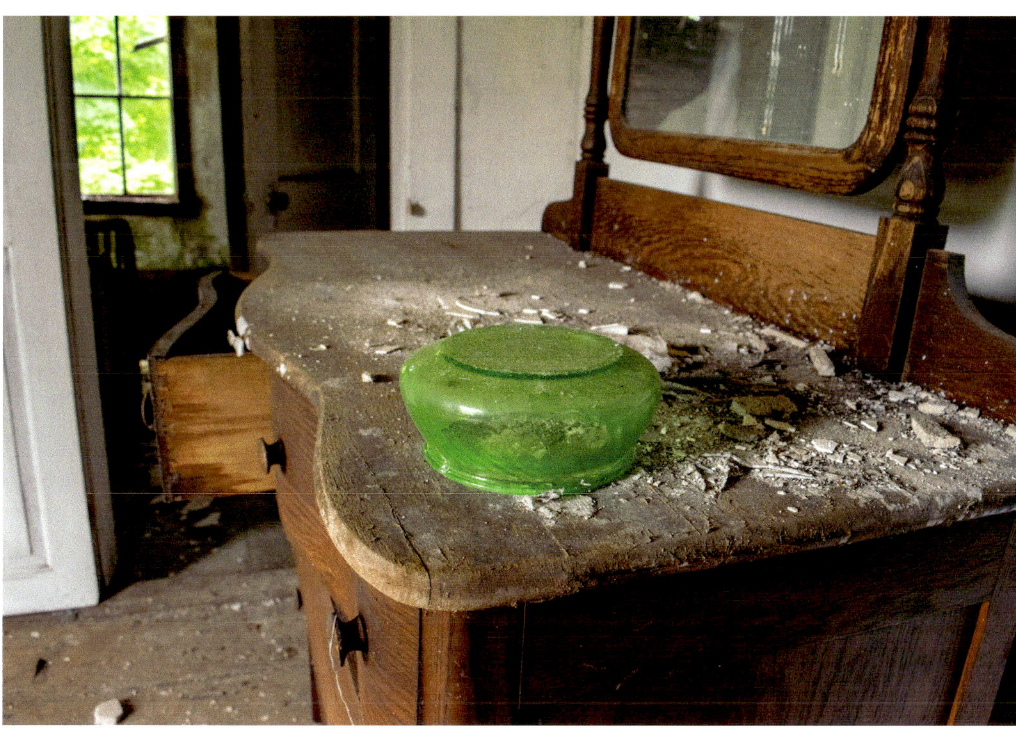

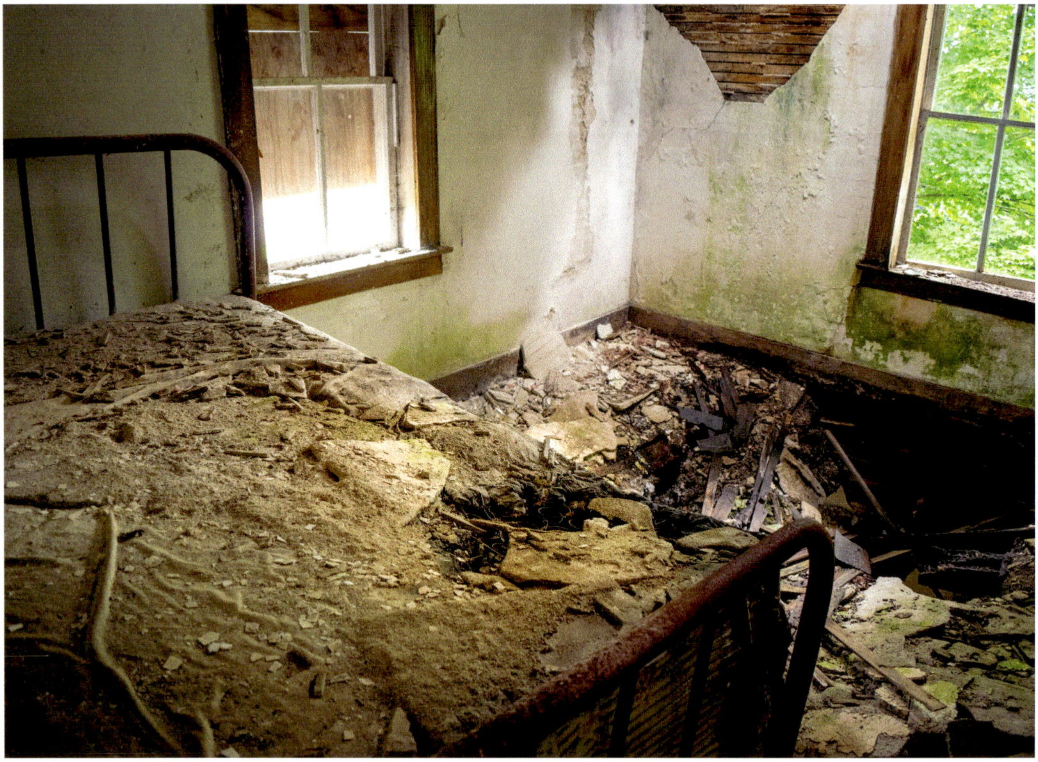

A metal-framed bed appears as if crouched in the corner, trying to avoid falling through the room's collapsing floor.

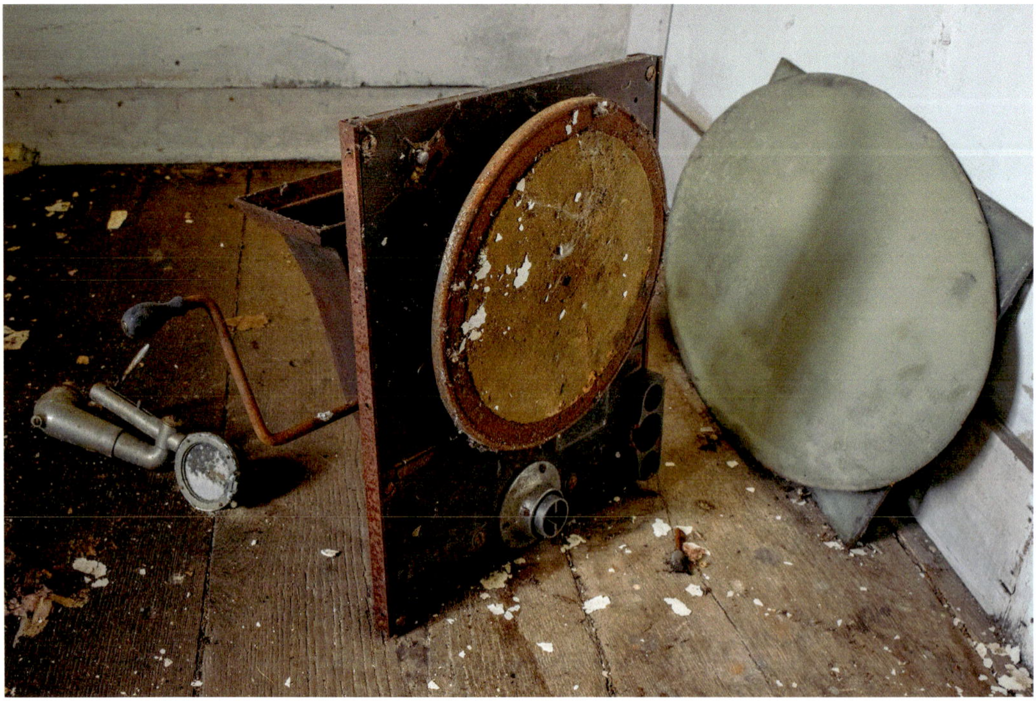

This 1920s tabletop phonograph is a bittersweet reminder of music and entertainment from the home's past life.

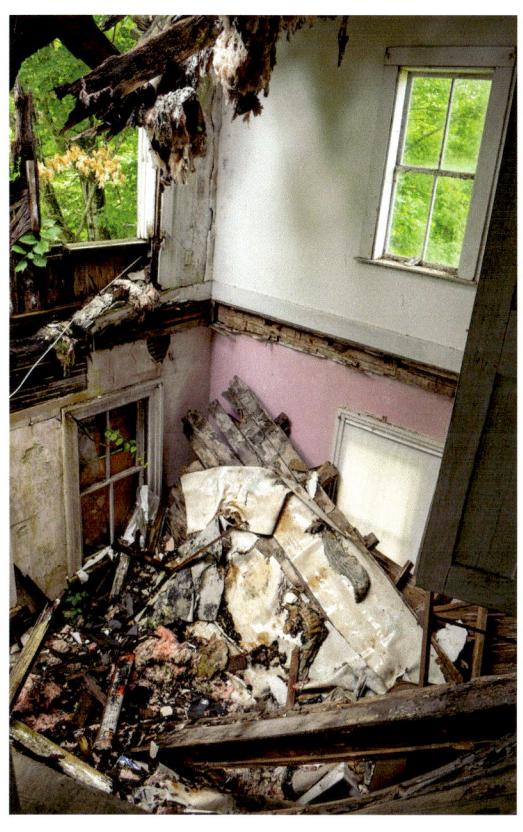

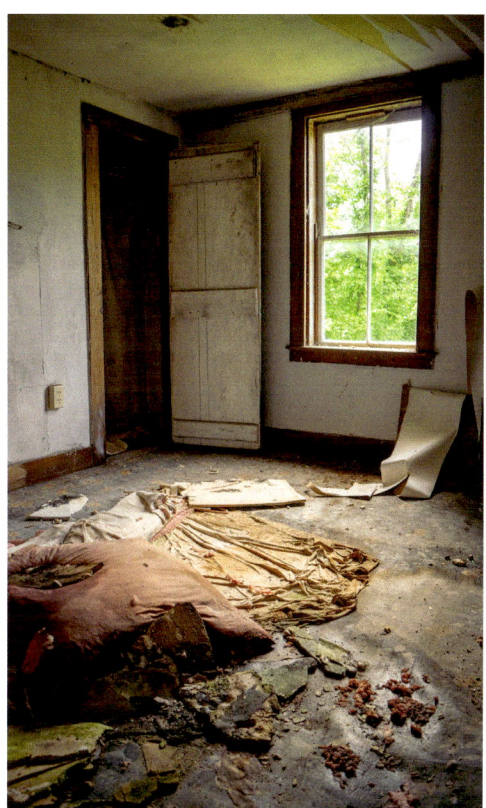

Above left: Shocking structural collapse has brought an upstairs bedroom down into the home's parlor, obscuring its cheerful pink walls.

Above right: A back bedroom with empty closet appears almost livable compared to the rest of the house.

Right: Looking down a treacherous central staircase with nicely turned balusters.

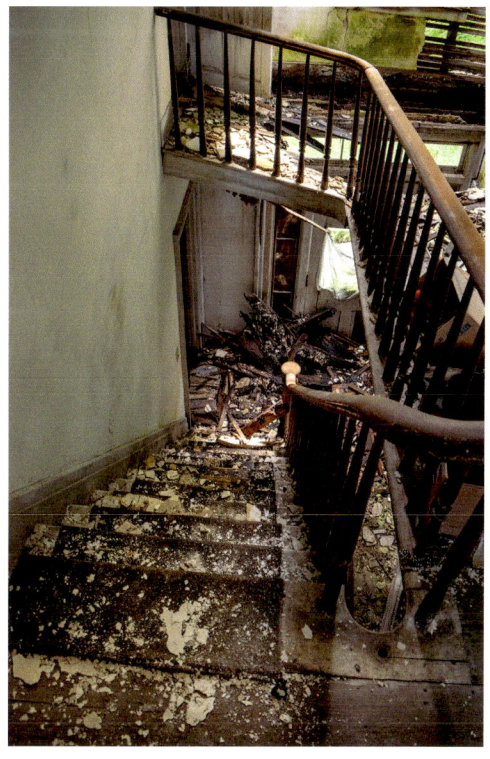

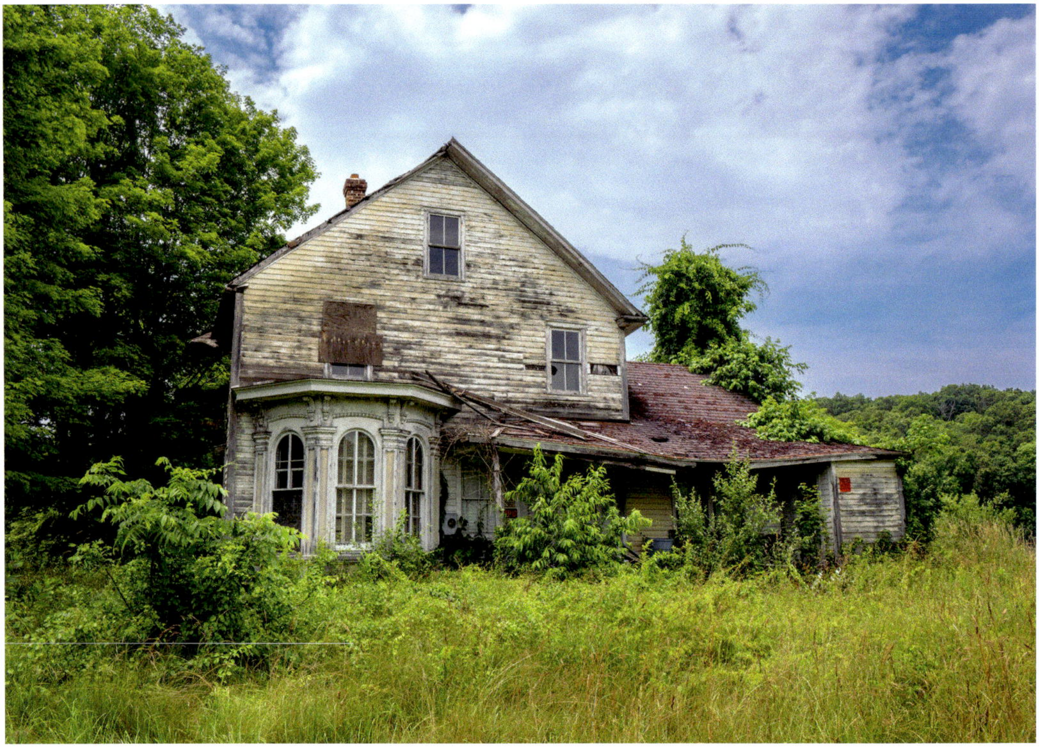

![A side view of the abandoned house with a canted bay window and collapsing porch, surrounded by overgrown vegetation.](image-top)

A side view of the house shows interesting architectural features, including an ornate canted bay window and collapsing farmer's porch.

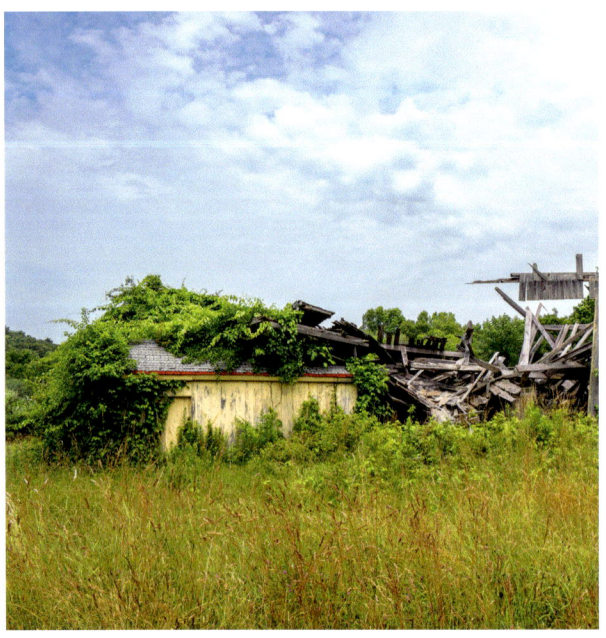

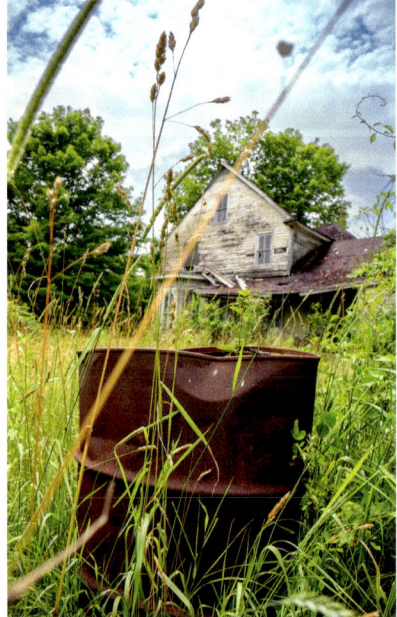

Above left: This pile of debris was a large, steeply pitched barn in the not-too-distant past.

Above right: A depth-of-field shot depicts one of several metal drums that mark the edge of the yard.

5

THE RIVERSIDE RUINS

Picturing the New England countryside might bring to mind rolling farmland, old houses, covered bridges, and other symbols of rural charm. Sometimes left out of the frame, though, are numerous early mills that dot the region's waterways, veritable forces of nature that harnessed hydropower to advance the Industrial Revolution. In particular, undeveloped areas of the Quiet Corner offered nineteenth-century textile barons the space and resources to build towering factories with plenty of room to expand. The corresponding boom in machine-based production had a lasting impact on both the state's economy and the map itself. A steady influx of laborers recruited to meet growing demand necessitated new housing, shops, and all manner of related infrastructure—including, in some cases, the creation of entire towns.

What survives of these mills varies from place to place. Some have been successfully redeveloped, some destroyed by time, while others remain perpetually vacant. In the case of this riverside ruin, what was once a monumental complex has been left to decay in the middle of a historic village that was founded to support its operation. The tributary that flows beside the overgrown site once supplied enormous energy capable of powering 1,750 looms, making the original facility here one of the largest of its kind in the world. Built during the 1850s, it employed over 1,000 people before, unfortunately, burning to the ground only thirty years after construction.

The vast potential of the location did not stay dormant for long—a subsequent mill was developed in 1901, an equally capable five-story behemoth dedicated to revitalizing local textile production. The business succeeded in supplying, among other things, military gear used in World War II, but its heyday was relatively short-lived. Having failed to escape New England's industrial decline across the first half of the century, it eventually shuttered for good in 1966.

Touring the crumbling buildings, now mostly devoid of machinery, showcases a long history of random use and exploration since it was abandoned, including stripped vehicles, trash from partygoers, and some memorable graffiti work that occasionally comments directly on the space's vibe. Though much of the ruin was demolished after yet another major fire in the late 1990s, what is left is a testament to the craftsmanship of period industrial architecture, highlighted by beautiful brickwork, imposing granite walls, and elegant arched windows. The remains of the hydropower system, including penstocks, a turbine, and other mechanisms, reflect impressive feats of engineering that once harnessed the river's natural forces to fuel a massive enterprise and, at one time, a village that still bears its name.

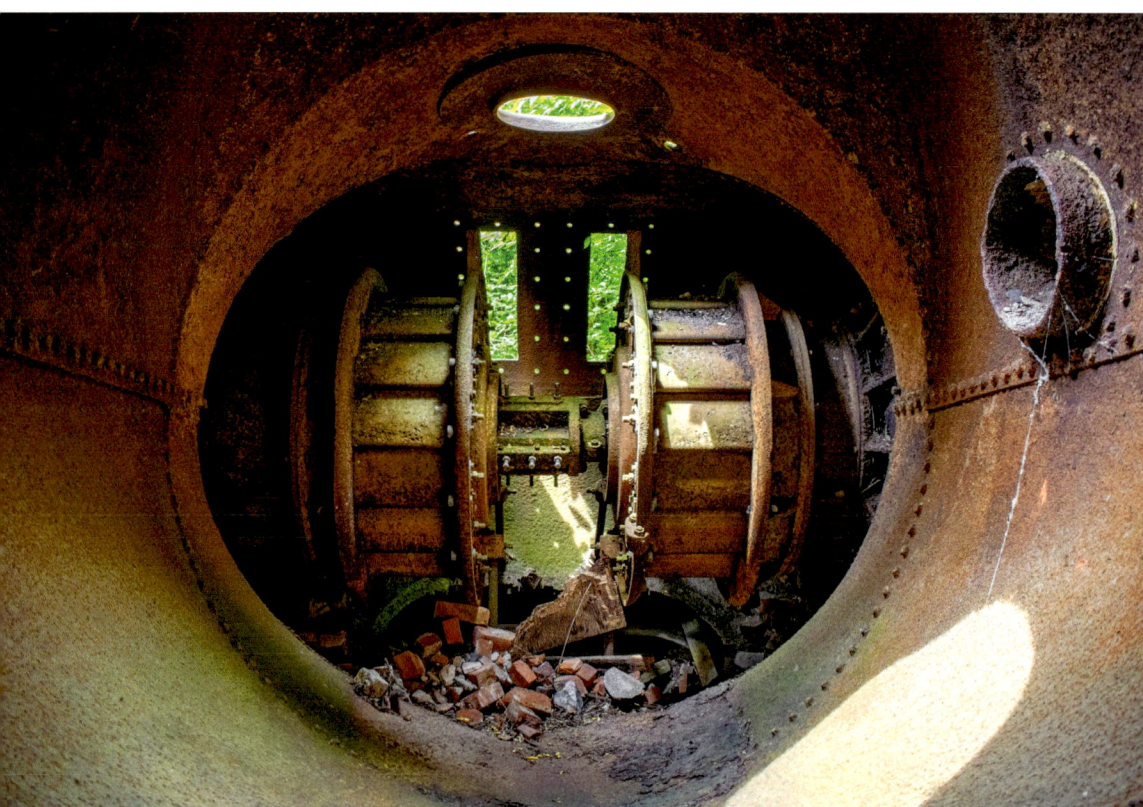

This massive turbine converted water from a nearby river into a power source for the complex.

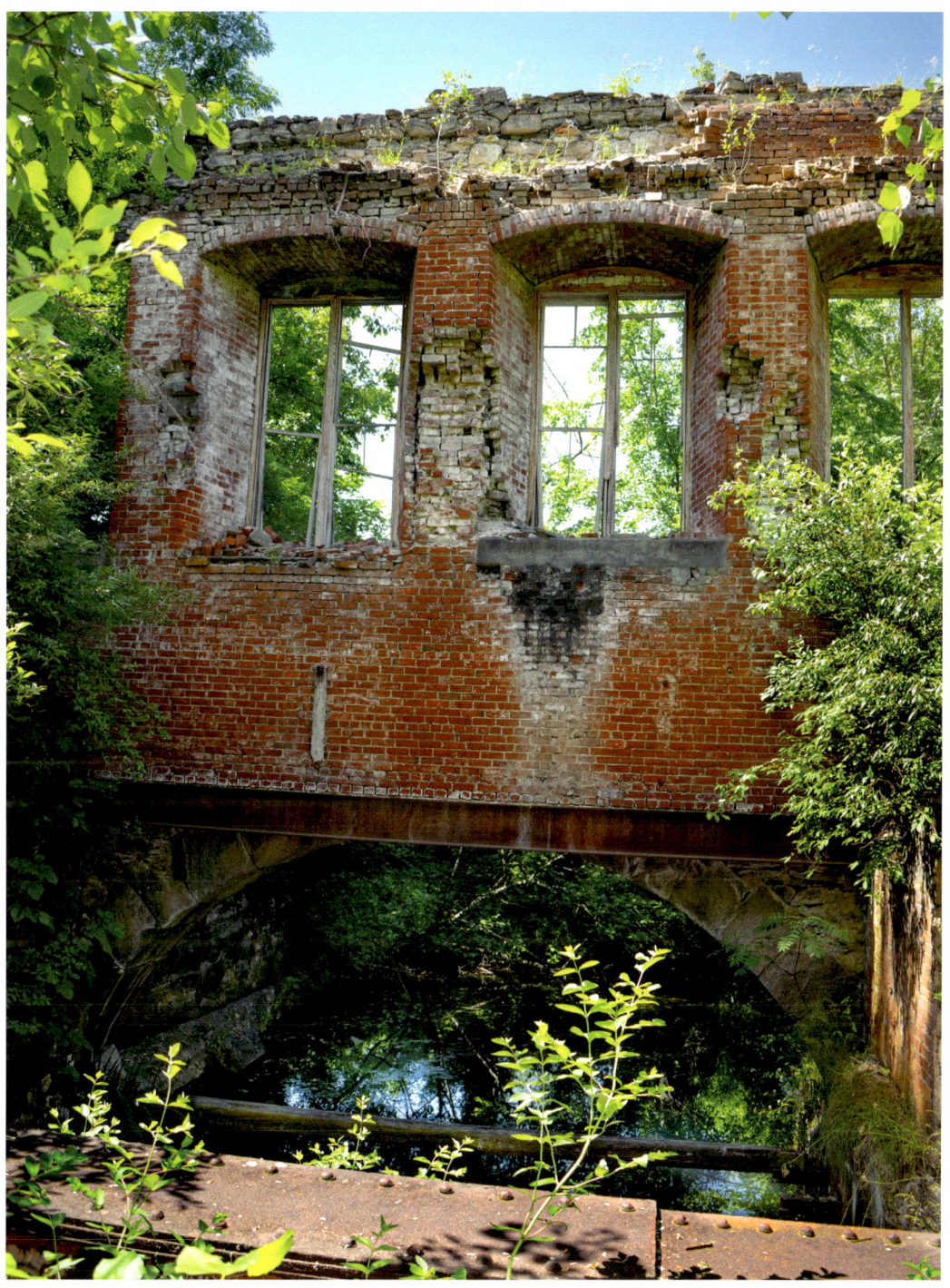

The remains of the mill's hydropower house feature beautiful brickwork and elegant windows. Water exited this building through a tail race, a channel visible beneath the archway.

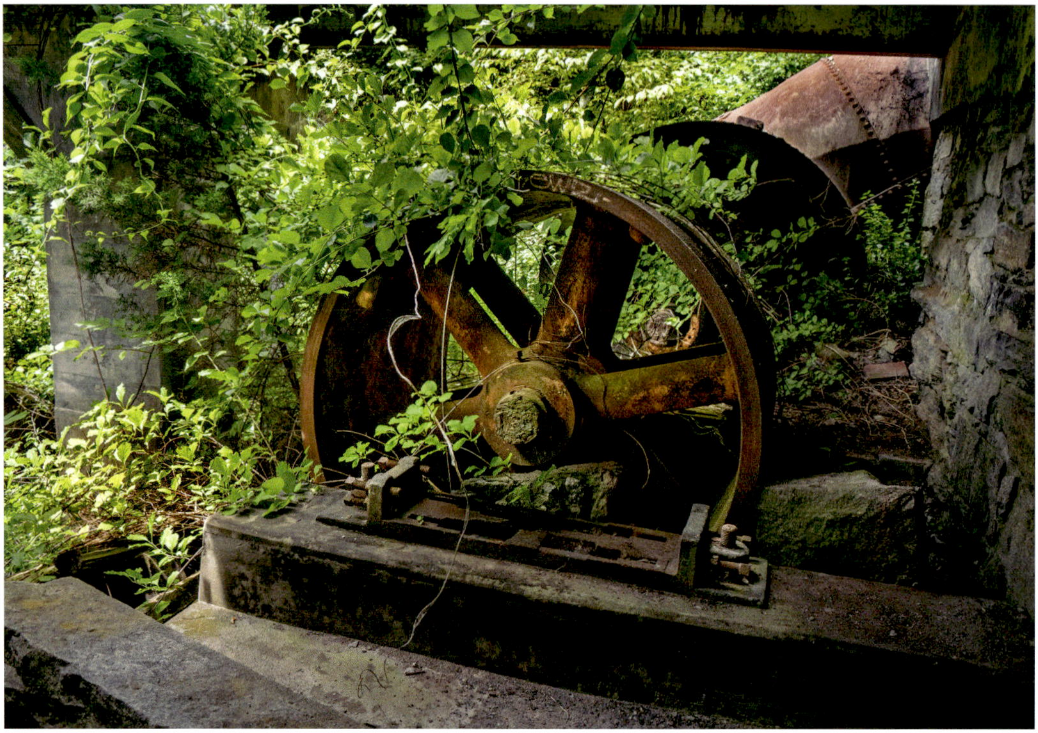

Vines tangle around a flywheel from the hydropower generation system.

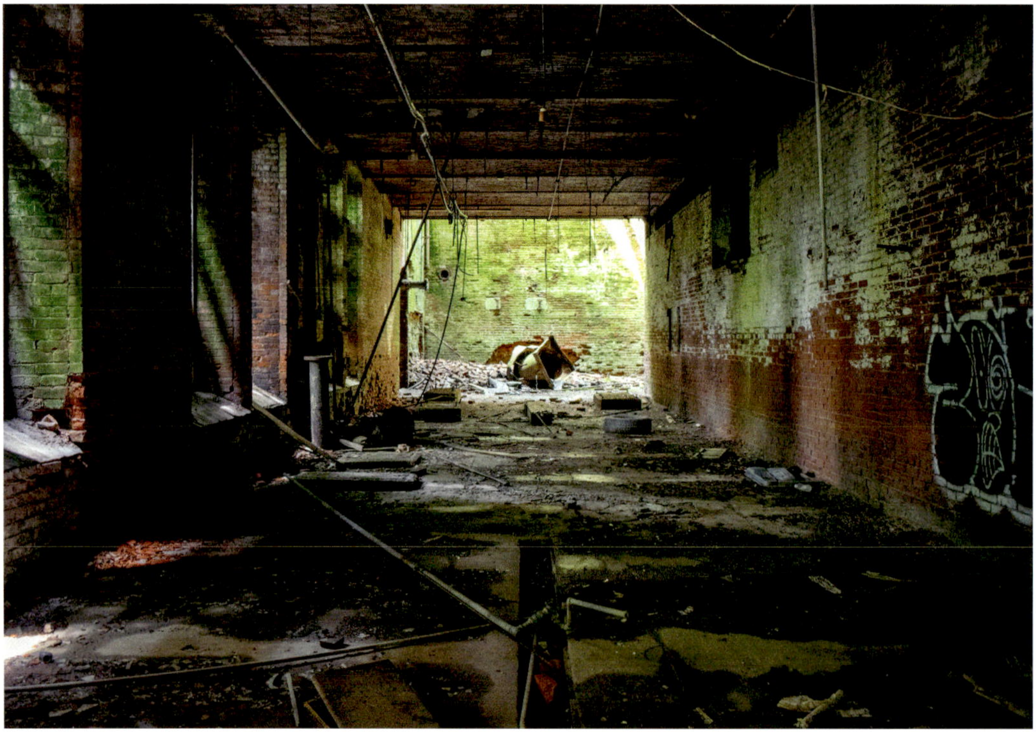

A wide passage within the mill's steam plant, where coal-powered boilers provided additional electricity and heat.

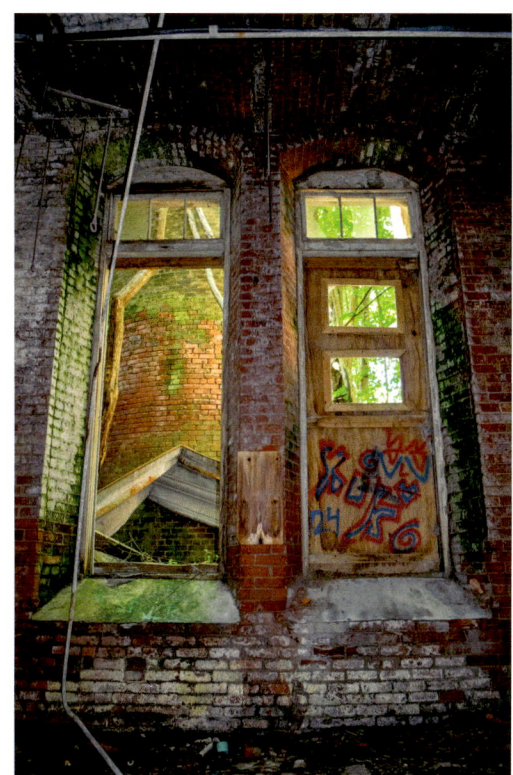

Right: Tall, slender arched windows line a dark hallway, giving the space a somewhat ecclesiastical feeling.

Below: Fallen ductwork and a concrete base are positioned like pieces of a modern art installation.

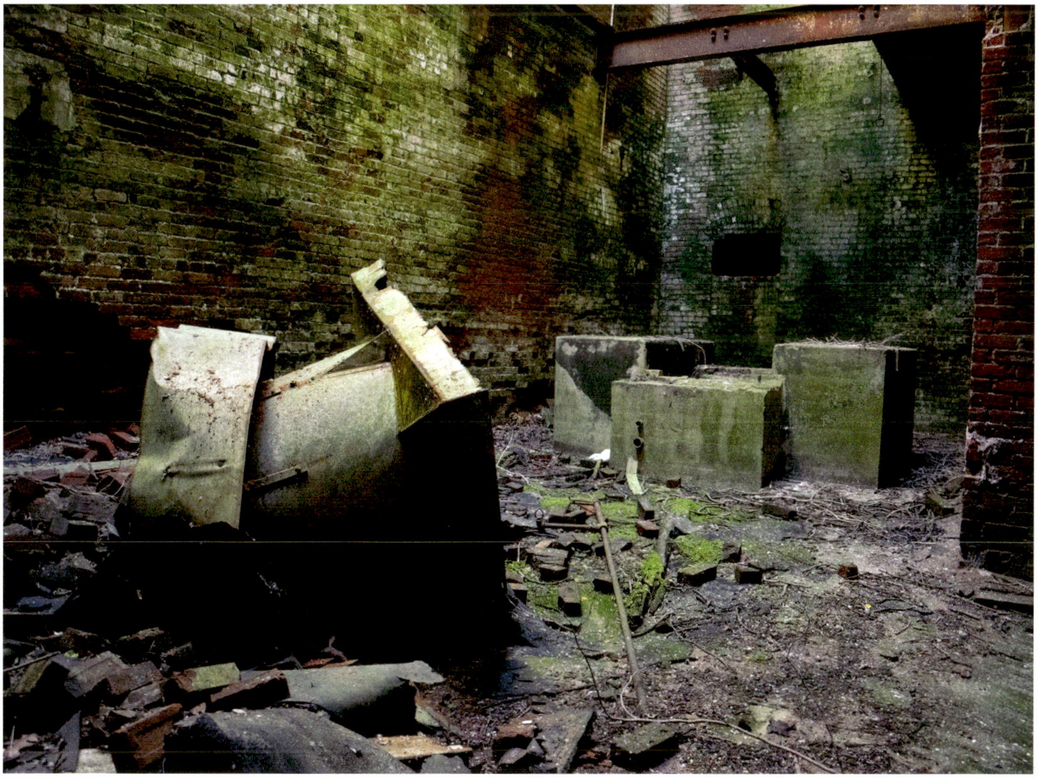

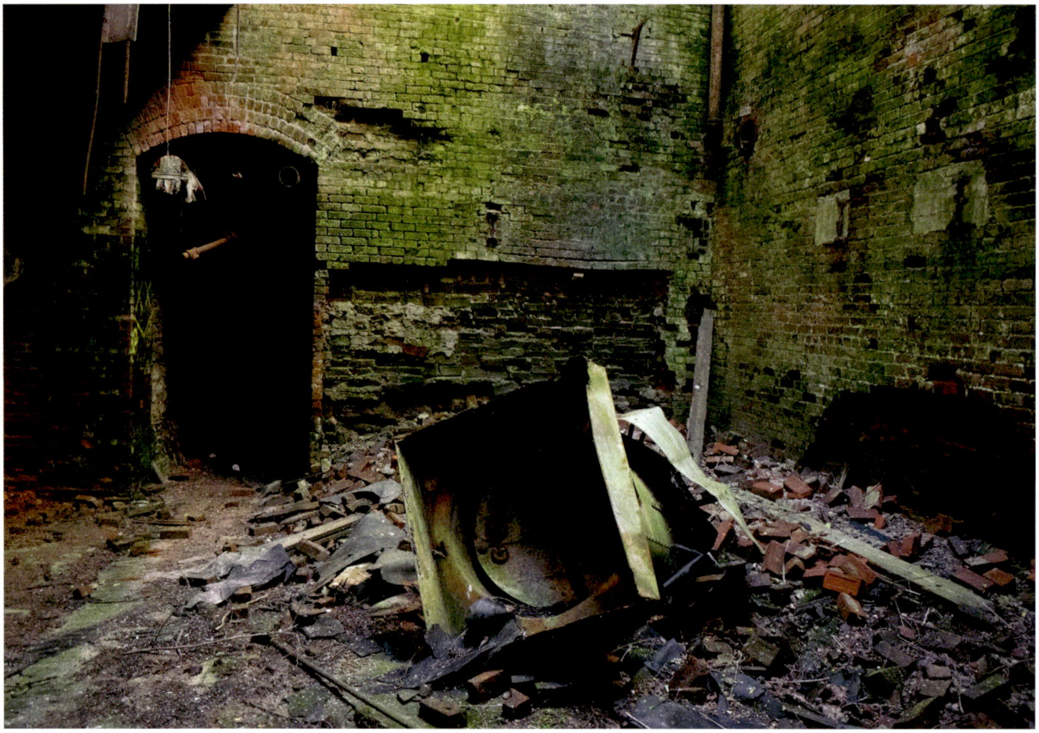

A dungeon-like atmosphere pervades this part of the facility.

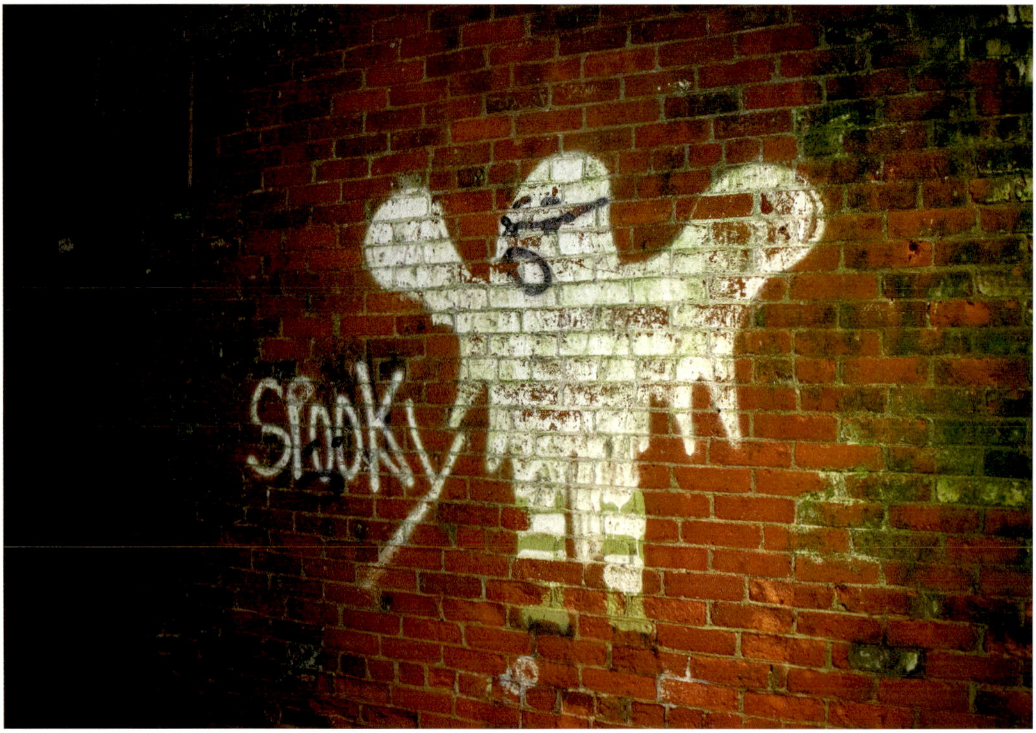

This graffiti accurately sums up the vibe here.

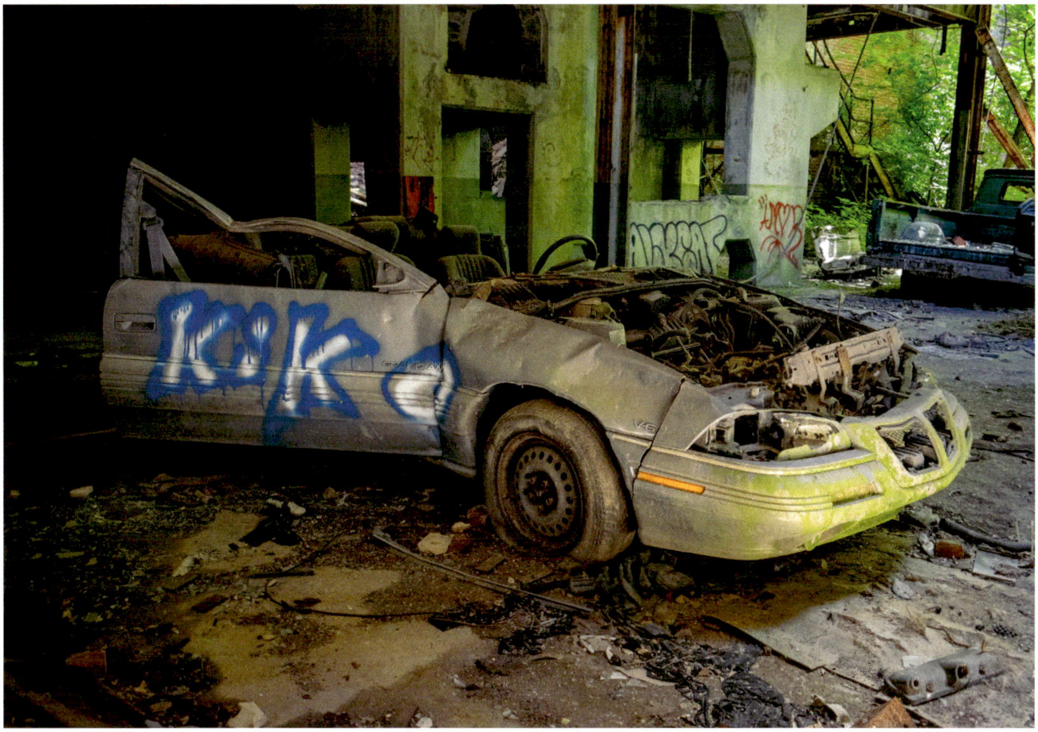

Several stripped and abandoned vehicles languish inside one of the remaining structures.

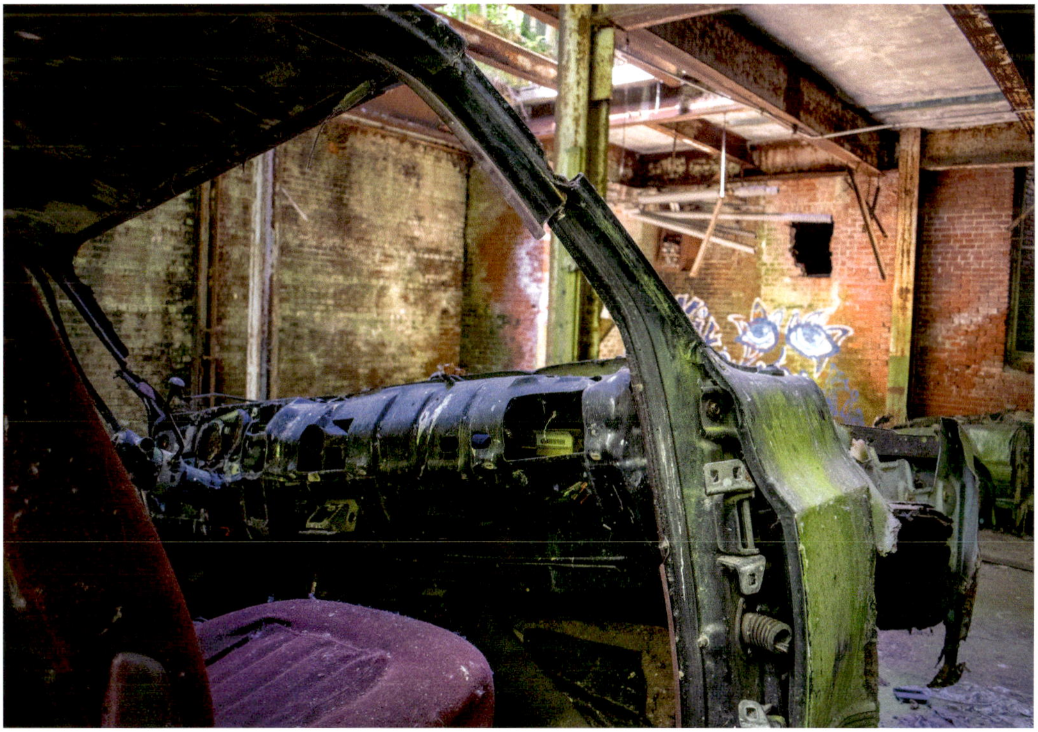

The dashboard might be mangled, but the upholstery of this vintage truck is surprisingly intact.

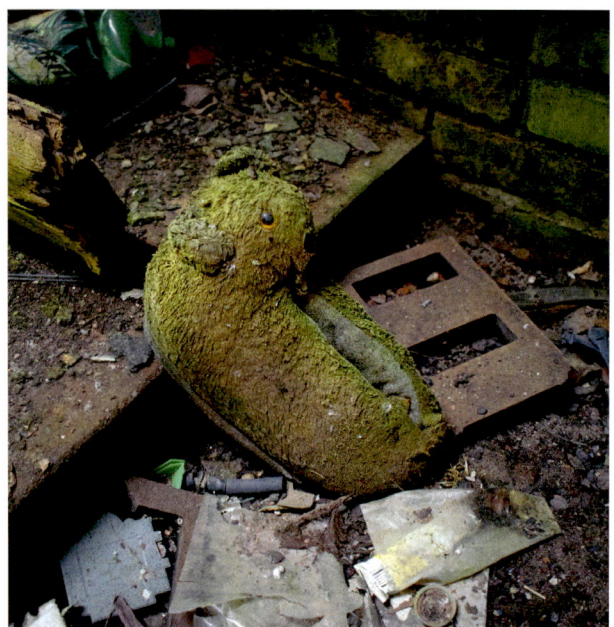
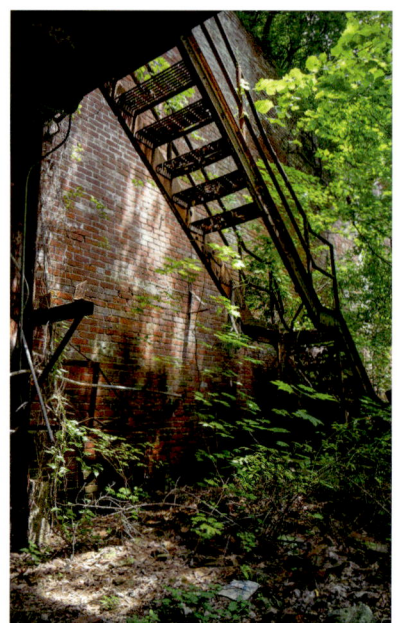

Above left: A single teddy bear slipper looks sad to have been left behind.

Above right: This staircase to the next level would not meet OSHA standards.

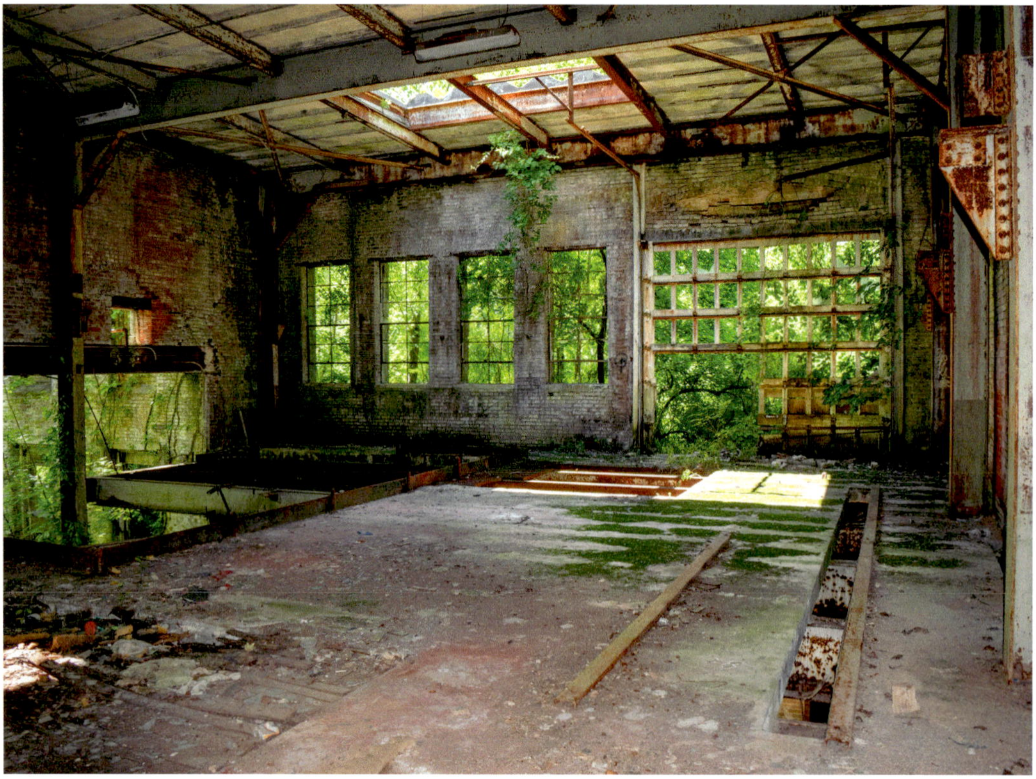

Tall trees obstruct the view from upper-floor windows, creating a verdant atmosphere.

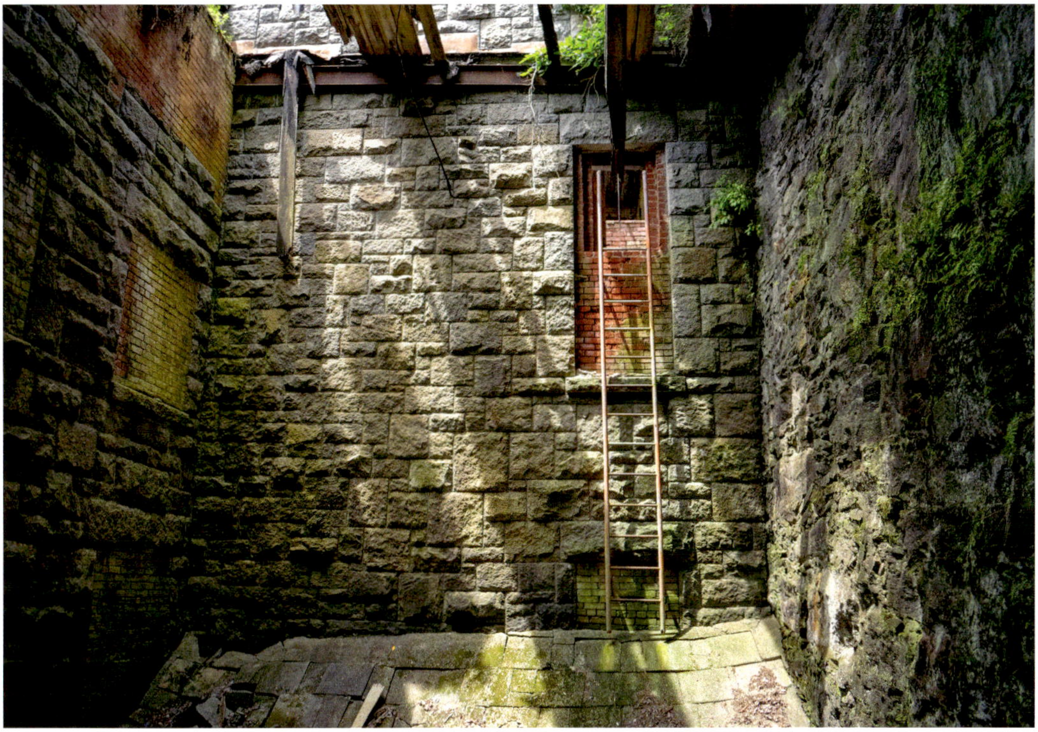

Above: A coal storage chamber. The room has an angled floor to keep contents moving toward the bottom as it is unloaded.

Right: One of two surviving smokestacks integral to the coal-powered steam plant.

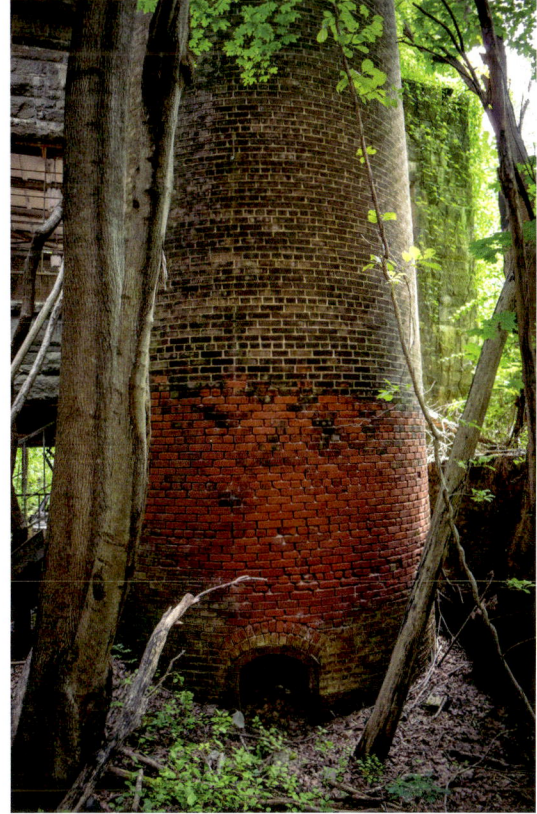

6

THE ABANDONED ACRES

Connecticut is home to over 5,000 farms, many of which are family affairs of modest size. In recent years, continuous pressure from out-of-state competitors, combined with labor shortages and waning interest from young people, has led to a steady decline in their numbers. Nevertheless, Eastern Connecticut maintains a long agricultural tradition across a wide variety of products, including milk, eggs, vegetables, and other staples. And it's not uncommon for Quiet Corner farmers to measure their history in terms of generations, even centuries.

But what happens when familial threads are broken, or financial challenges make it impossible to carry on? Too often, unfortunate terms such as "redevelopment" and "subdivision" cast their shadows over the future of unspoiled acreage that is so integral to the region's historic character. Some properties that escape this fate simply end up abandoned, their farmsteads joining the ranks of countless relics that peek out from the edges of fields, lending rustic charm to scenic roads for as long as they manage to hold out against the elements. Others sit somewhere in between, occupying an uncertain limbo.

This chapter features a group of derelict buildings that once served a sizable 150-acre dairy and corn farm. A family business that finally came to its natural end, it has since been acquired by a local corporation for undetermined purposes, its destiny up in the air. While some activity still exists in the form of incidental haying in nearby fields, the central complex has transformed into an underutilized site of striking proportions. Only time will tell whether the surrounding land endures as a block of quiet countryside or becomes the latest spot overrun with condos or commercial space.

On approach, towering silos are all that is initially visible amid the dense overgrowth, giving the impression of ancient ruins rising above the canopy of a jungle. As tall as these structures are, persistent vines have successfully reached the highest points, obscuring much of their rusted forms during the summer months. Interestingly, one steel silo has managed to retain its roof, while the second has found itself open to the air for a number of years—apparently creating perfect conditions for moss to spread an otherworldly bright-green carpet over the floor.

Climbing through the brush and into a warehouse-sized barn, the scale of the place comes into focus, along with a distinct feeling of emptiness. A few pieces of vintage farm machinery, left here in a state of frozen operation, barely make a dent in its storage capacity. Among the highlights is a beautiful 1970s-era tractor pulling two large trailers stacked high with bales. Not far away, an angry-looking mower and matching baler sit ready for duty. Also encountered are decaying storerooms, mostly stripped to the bone, and the strange sight of a beach chair with a matching rubber ducky (perhaps left behind from some past visitor's photo shoot). Like a slowly sinking island, the neighboring outbuildings and sheds have either burned down due to arson or reached various stages of collapse. Now only the central building and its silos remain fully standing, awaiting whatever fate that eventually comes to cull them from the landscape.

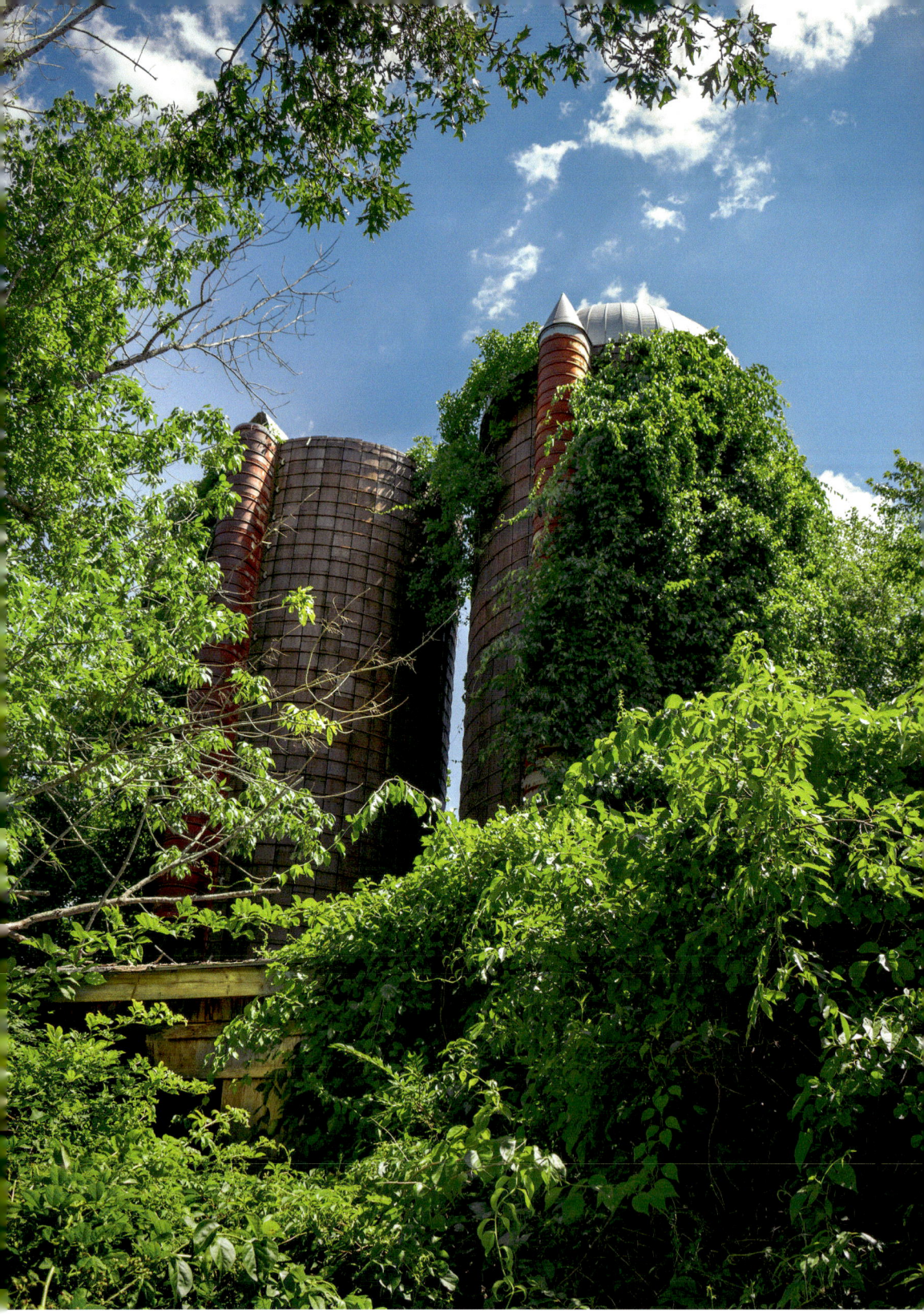

Towering silos rise above the overgrowth like ancient ruins.

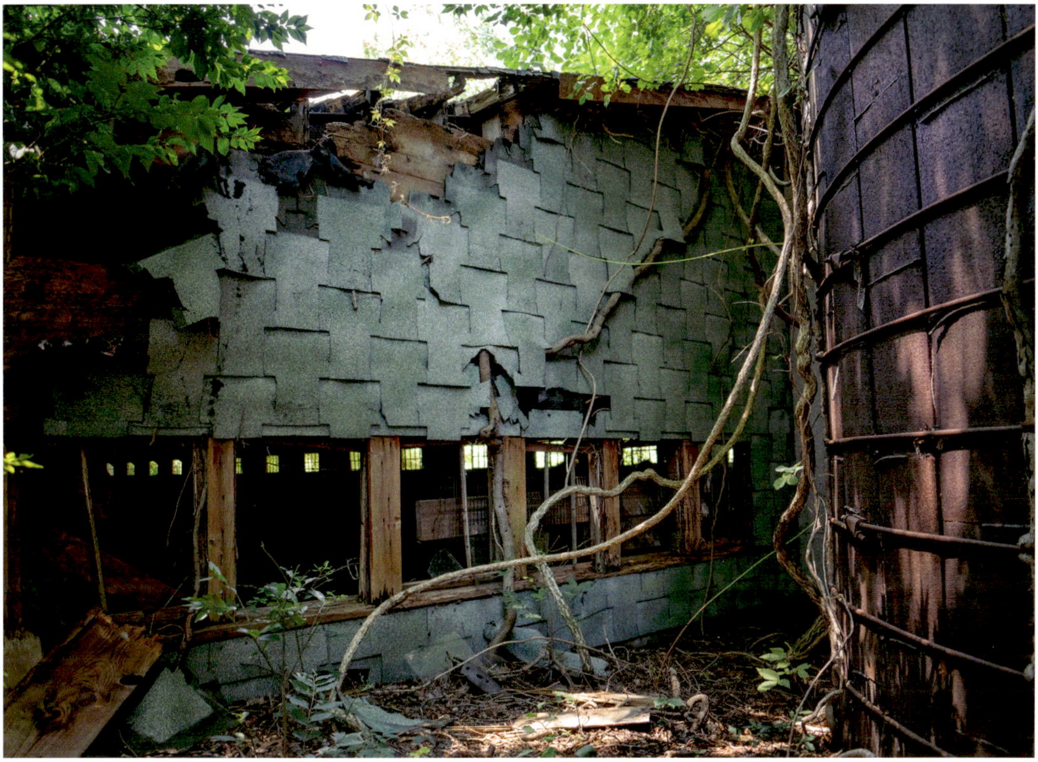

The main barn is far larger than it appears on approach.

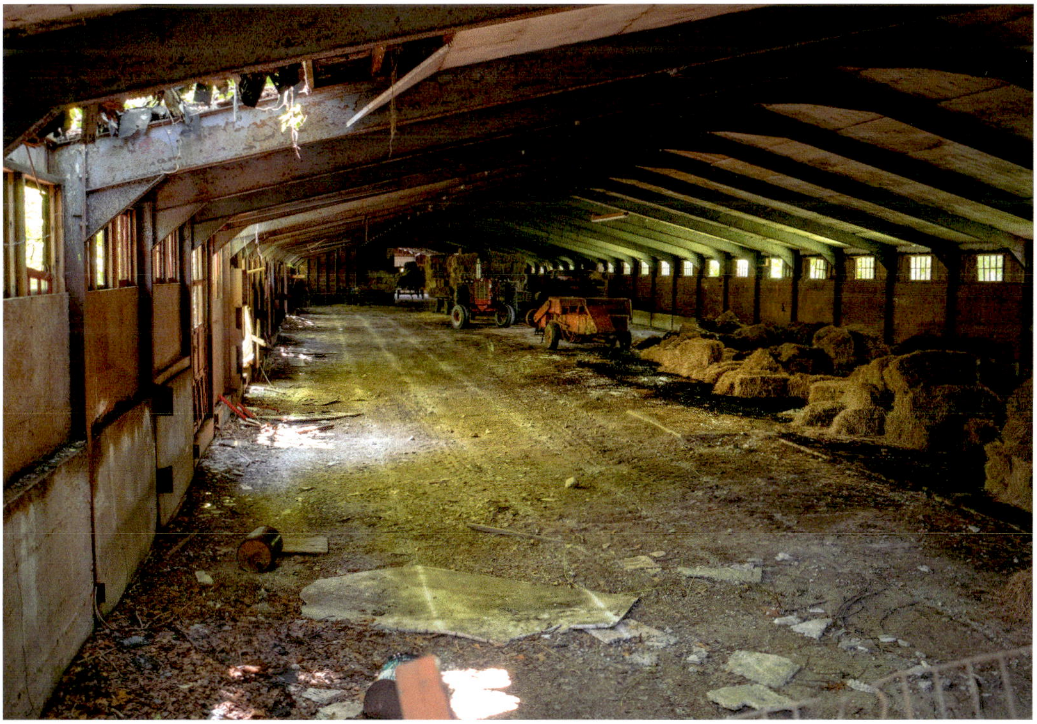

This warehouse-sized space could fit a large fleet of farm equipment and clearly a great deal of hay.

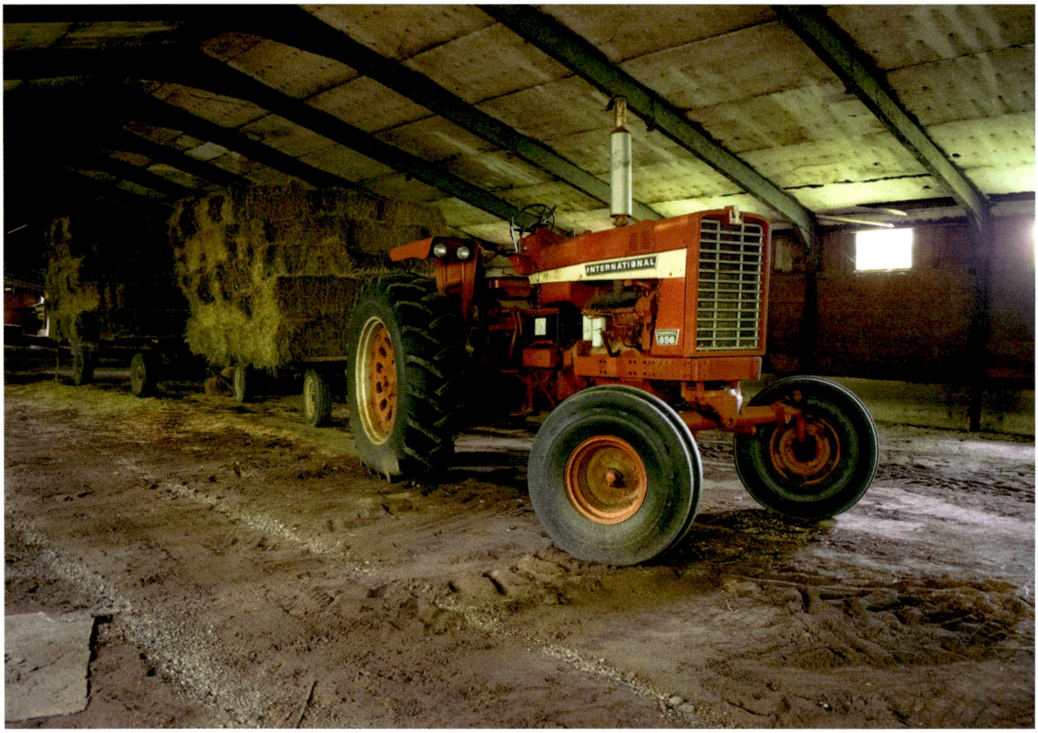

A vintage 1970s International Harvester brand tractor is the star of the show.

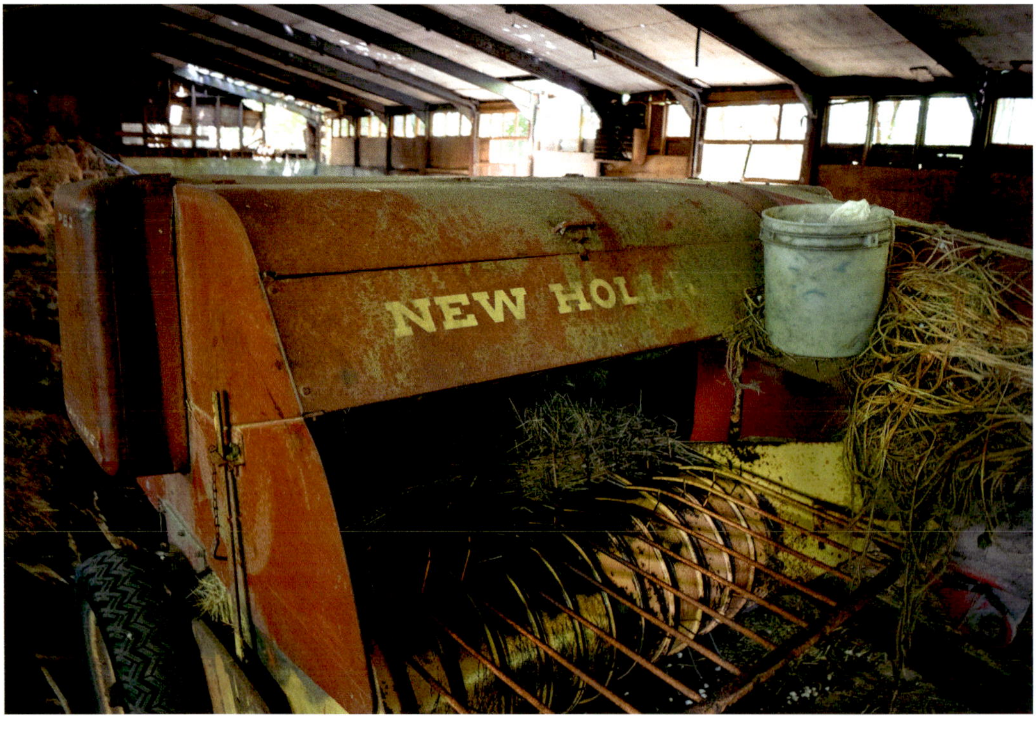

This big, red hay bailer looks ready for its next meal.

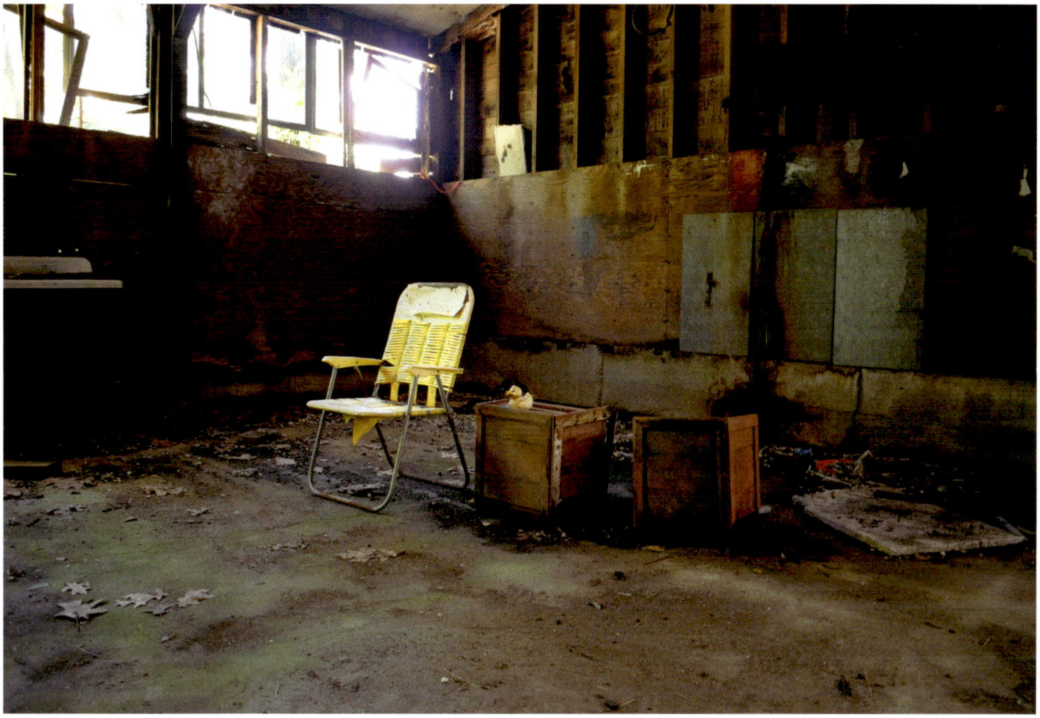

You never know what you will find exploring a vacant building. A yellow beach chair and matching rubber ducky look suspiciously like the remains of someone else's photo shoot.

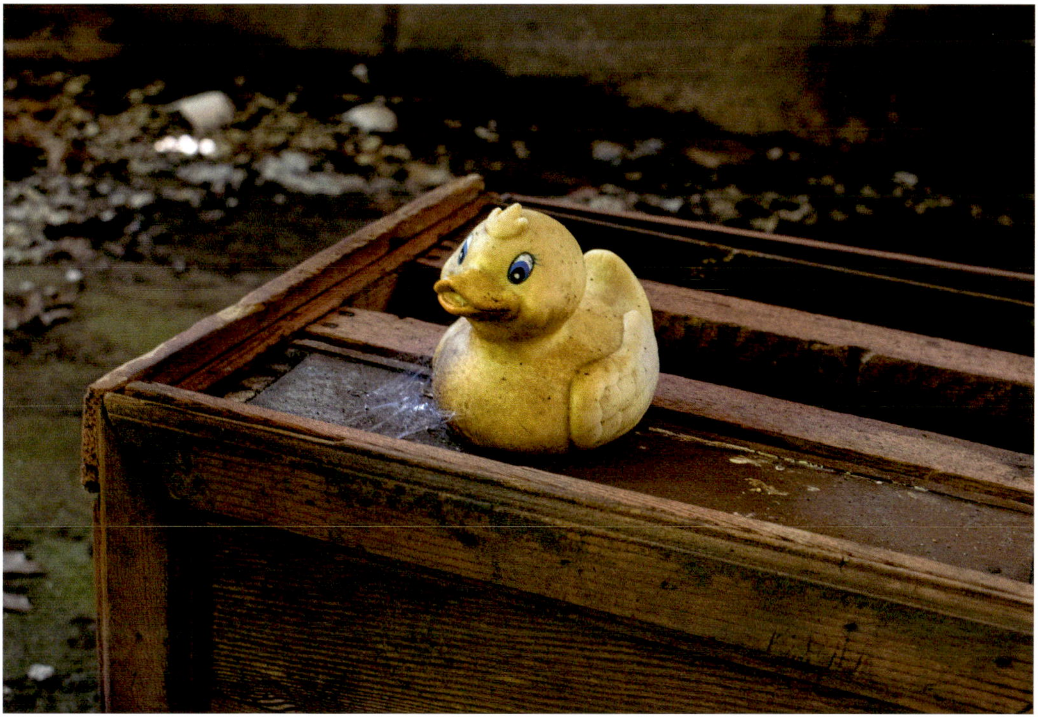

A cobwebbed rubber ducky stands out amid the gloom.

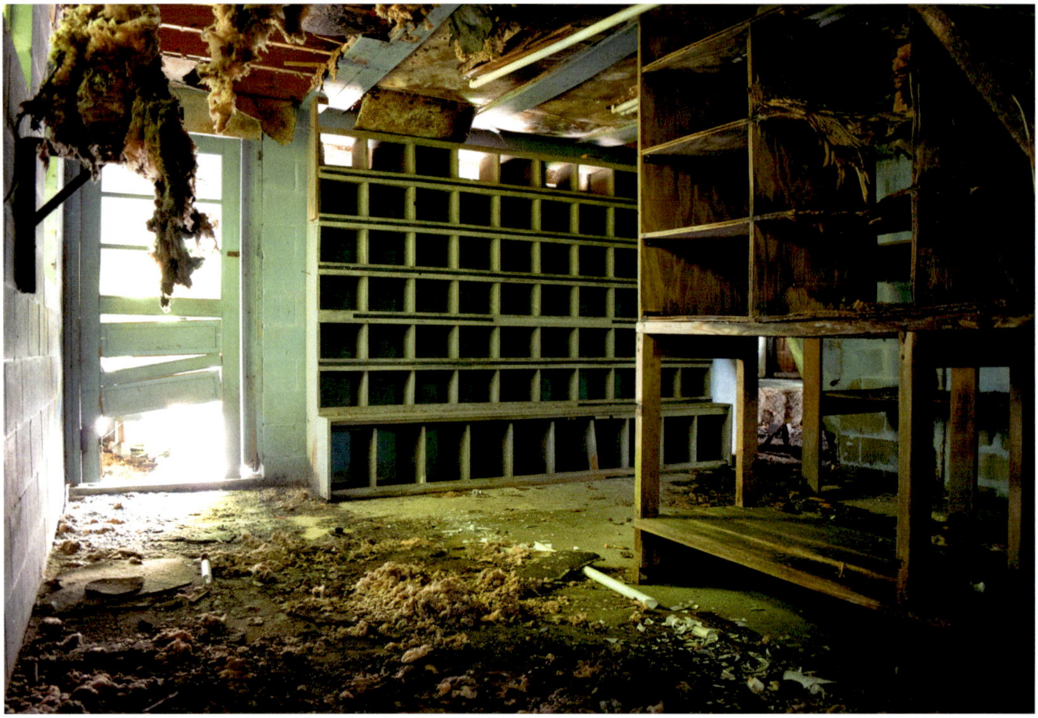

Likely a storeroom or workshop, this space features a variety of custom shelving—and decay.

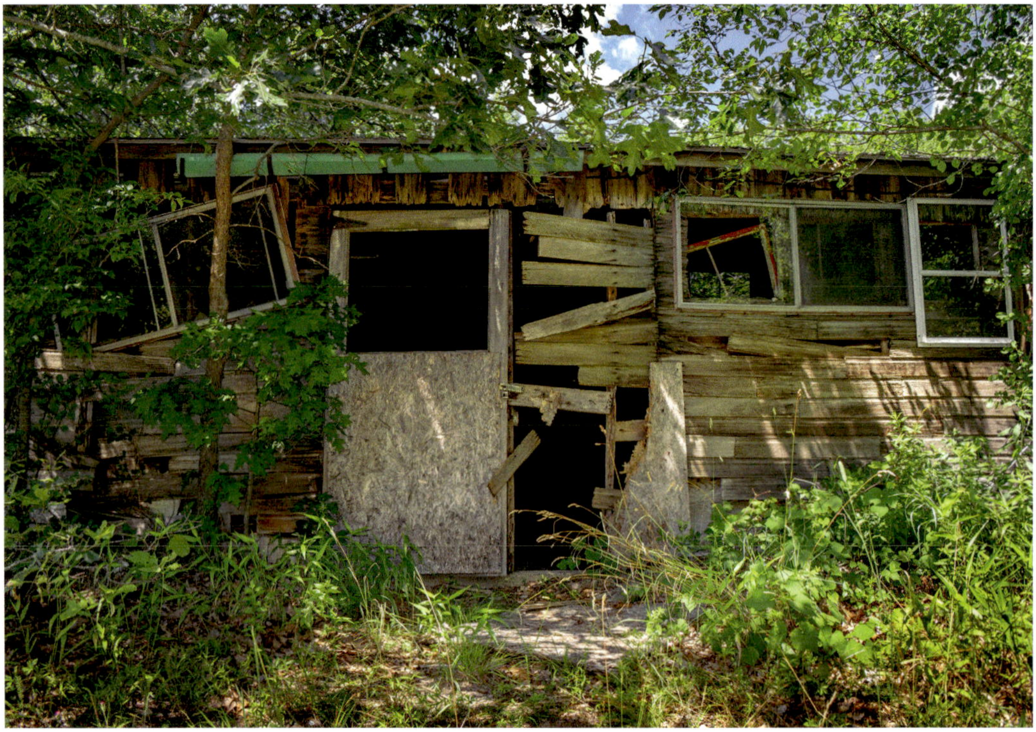

One of the entrances has deteriorated into a ramshackle mess.

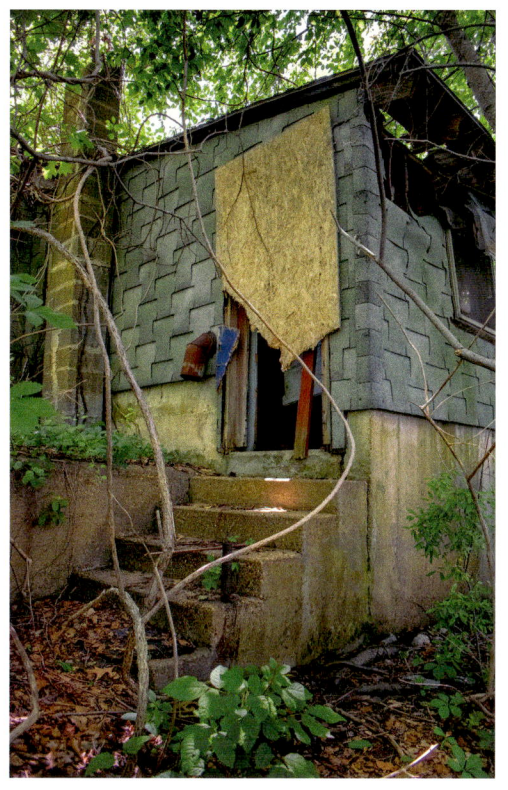

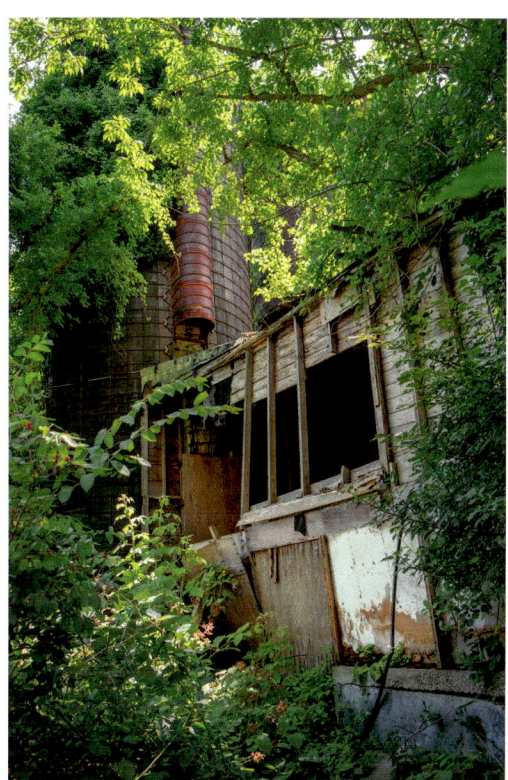

Above left: It has been a long time since anything was kept out of this doorway.

Above right: This crumbling loading dock gives access to the farm's massive silos.

Right: Persistent vines have managed to summit the towering structures.

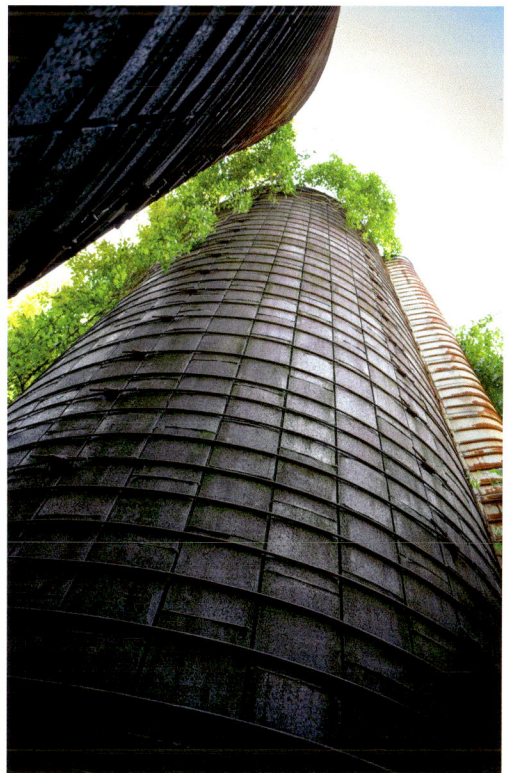

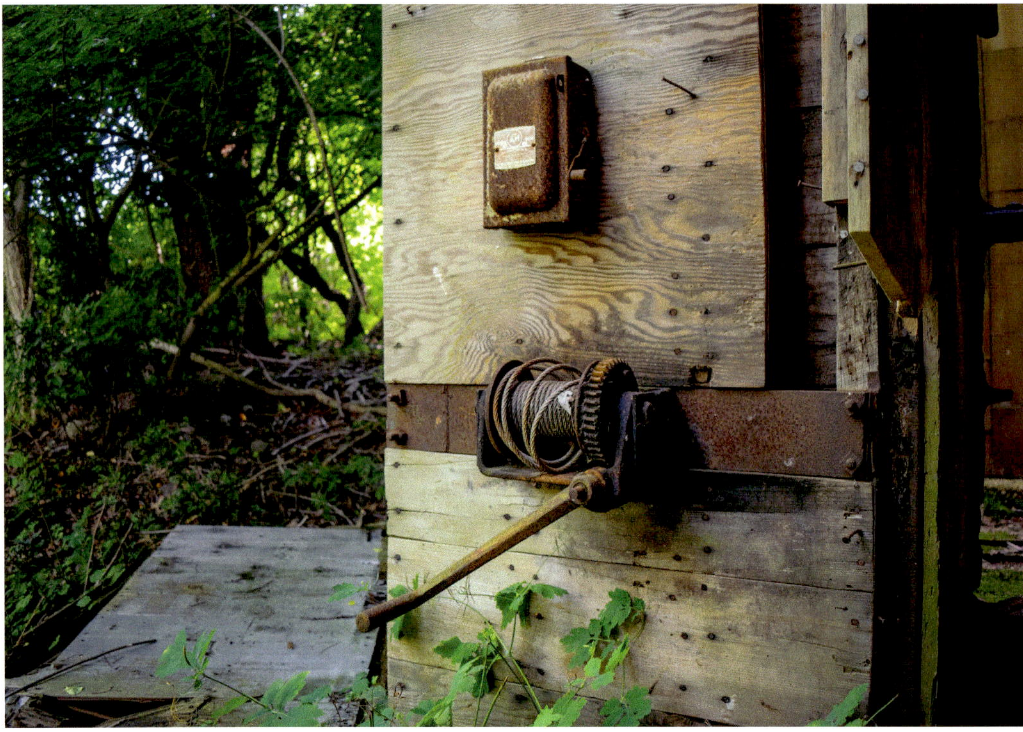

An old winch system, possibly used to raise or lower the position of a silo unloader machine.

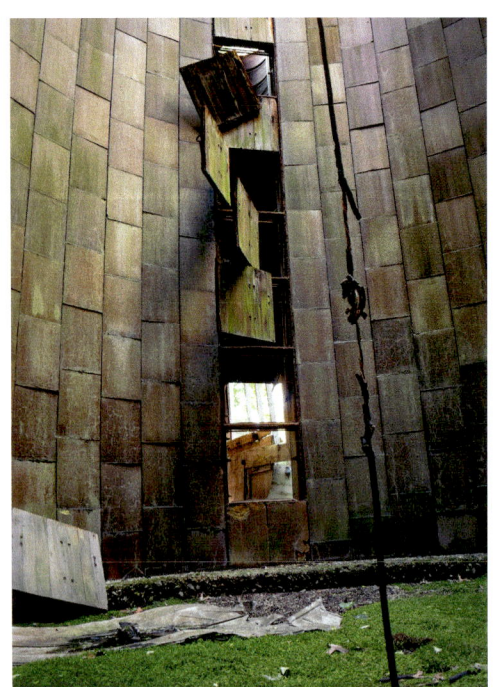

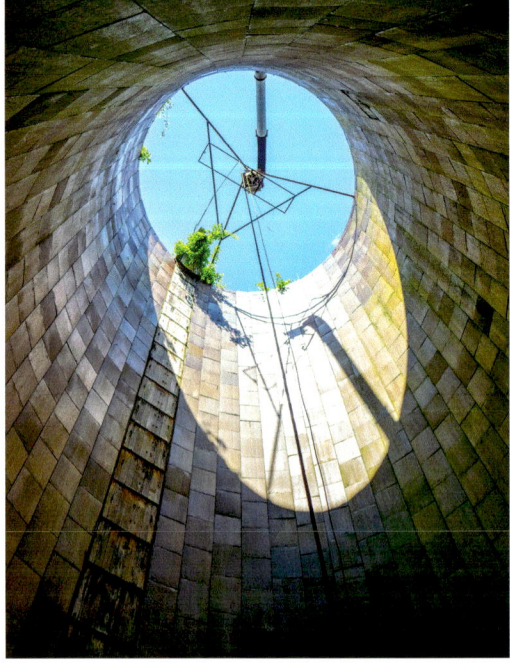

Above left: Beautiful green moss covers a silo floor, seeming to glow in the pleasant midday light.

Above right: This steel "bullet" silo is missing its top, revealing a bright blue summer sky above.

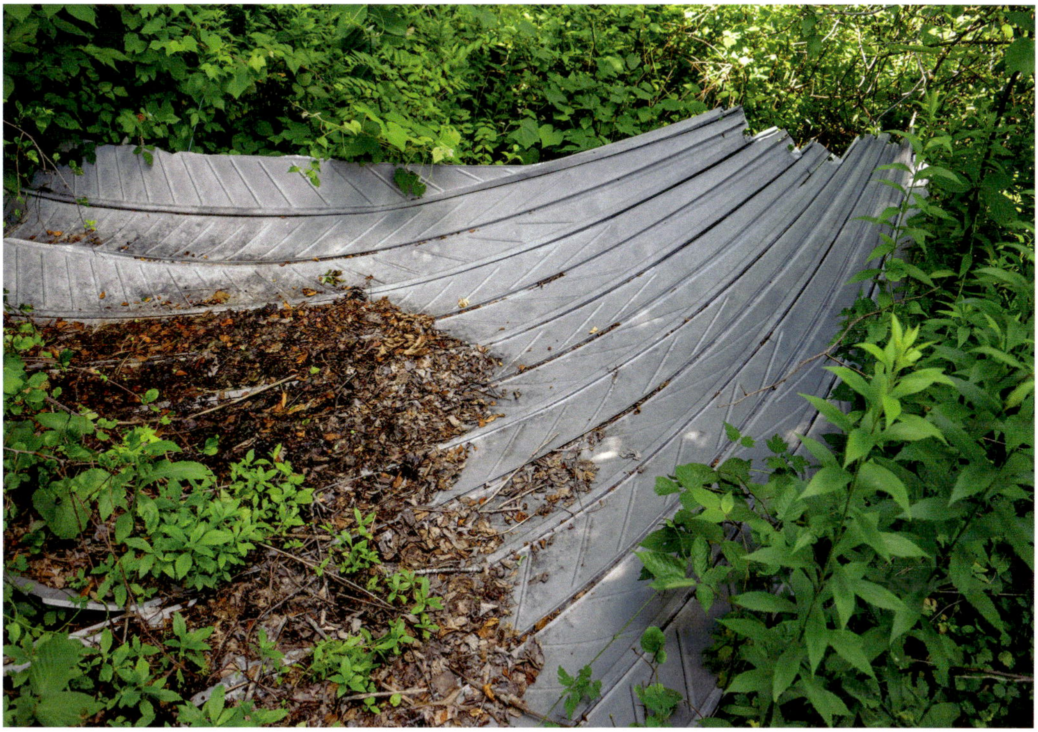

A piece of the missing silo roof sits outside among the brush, perhaps blown off in a storm.

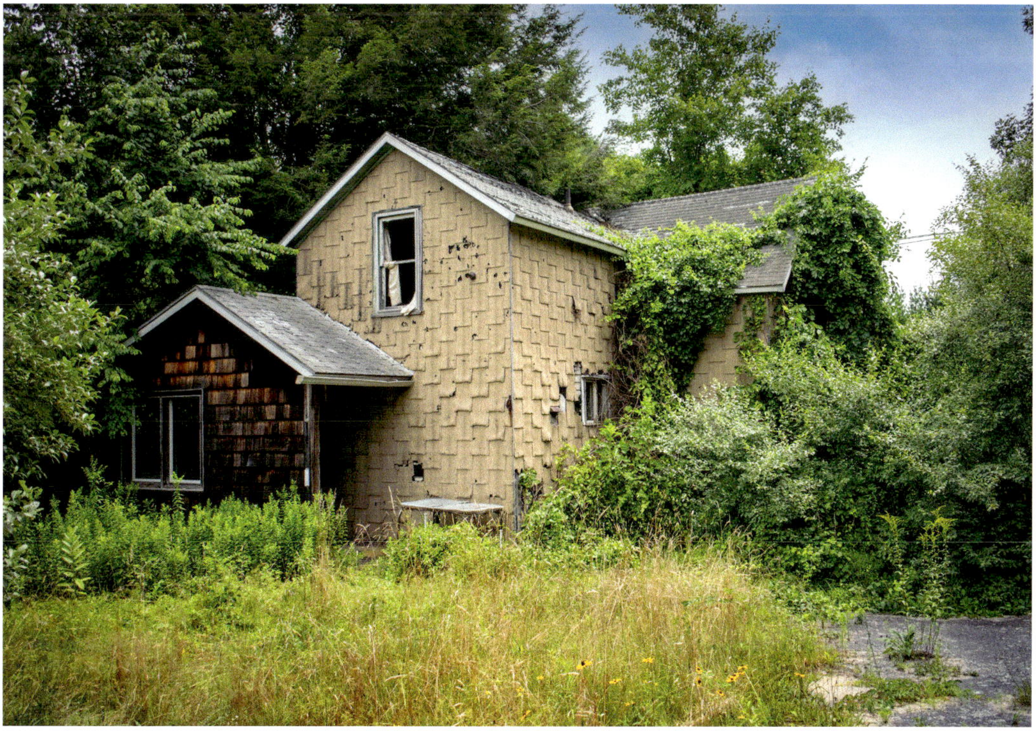

The adjacent farmhouse is a lonely sight, no doubt full of distant memories.

7

THE GREEN GETAWAY

This abandoned cabin feels perfectly at home in the woods of the Quiet Corner, where hunting, camping, and other outdoor pursuits remain popular with locals and tourists alike. As a comfortable base from which to fish, hike, or enjoy the area's natural beauty, it's easy to imagine it was once a relaxing getaway. In addition to respectable amenities, the creative construction and vibrant hues hint at a soulful builder who embraced the cheerful greens and yellows of the surrounding environment. Other touches, such as a brightly painted bench and a unique stained-glass window adorning the front door, complete a peaceful, welcoming scene.

Inside, the color theme continues with matching blinds that cast a warm, if somewhat eerie, verdigris glow across piles of decaying furniture. Despite its deteriorated state, the living space contains everything you might associate with modern glamping, from a mattress bed and wood-burning stove to a small kitchen area—along with all the board games you need to pass a quiet evening under the trees. On a chest of drawers in one corner, a vintage clock attests that, however long ago, this charming home away from home wound down at 5:52.

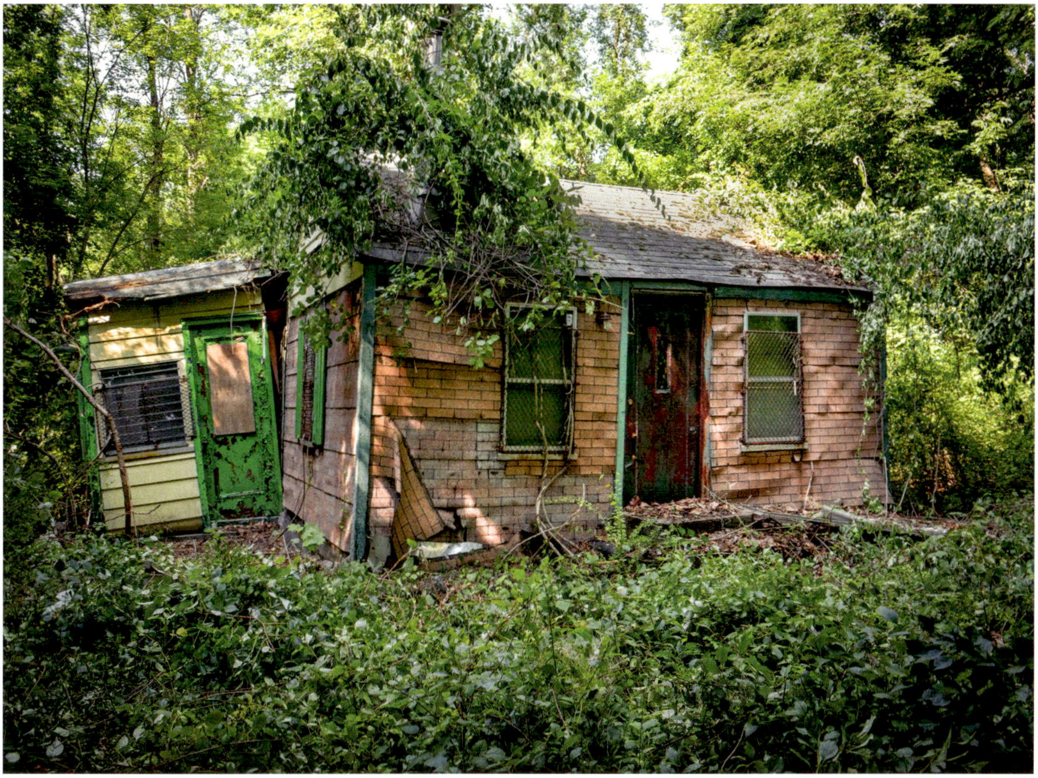

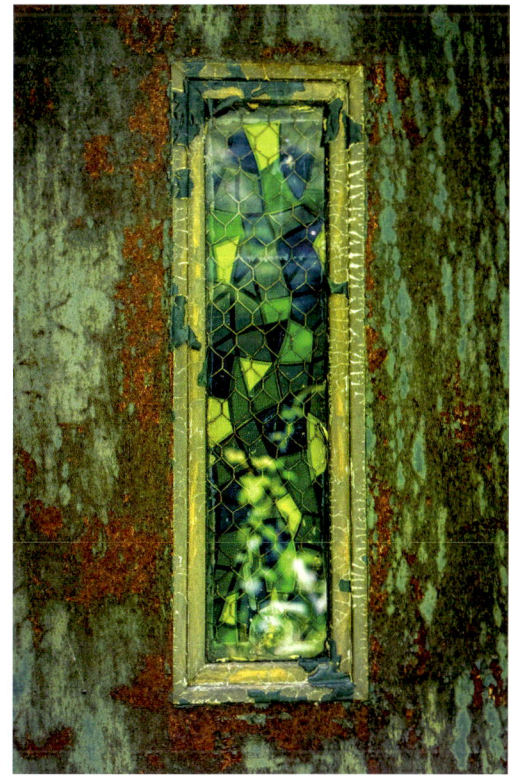

Above: The cabin's charming, bespoke design still shines through despite advanced deterioration.

Right: A cheerful stained-glass window adorns the front door, clearly chosen to match the building's color scheme of greens and yellows.

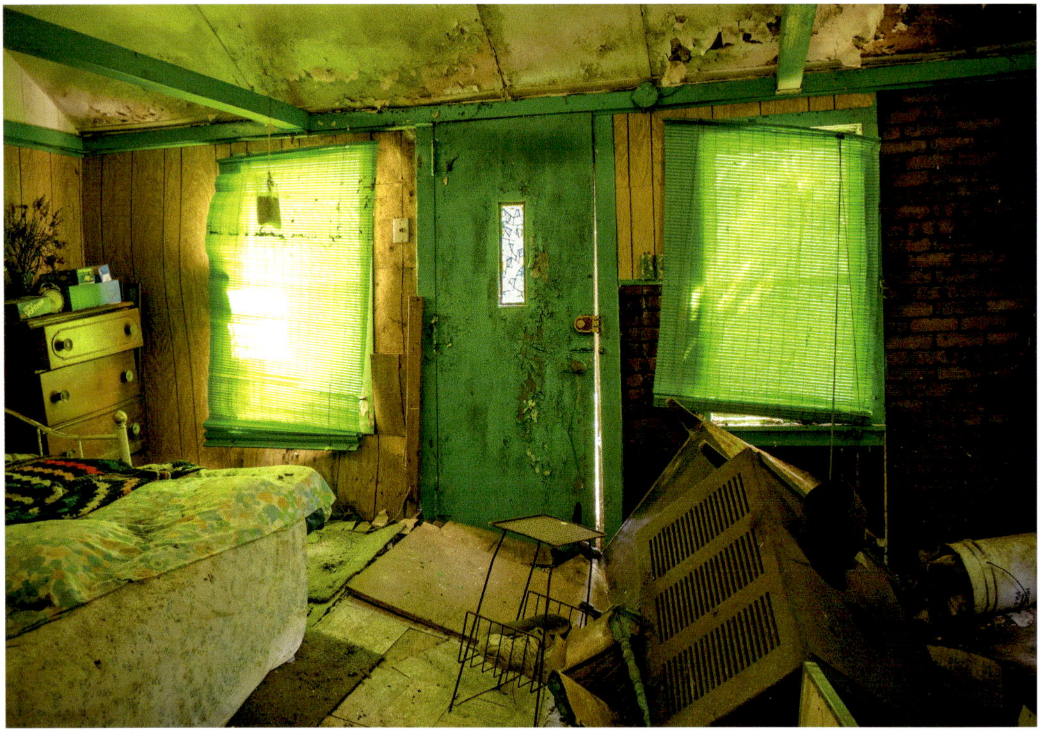

Faux bamboo blinds cast an eerie green glow across the main living space, where various fixtures and pieces of furniture have begun to fall through the collapsing floor.

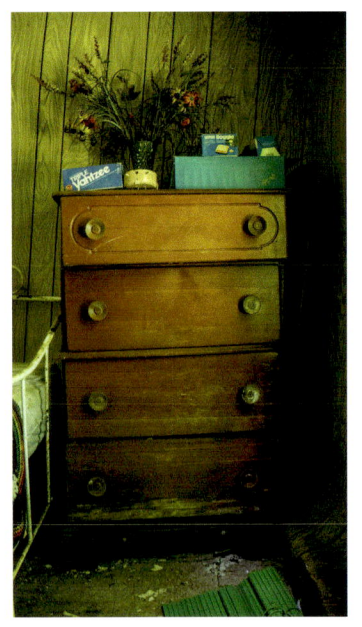 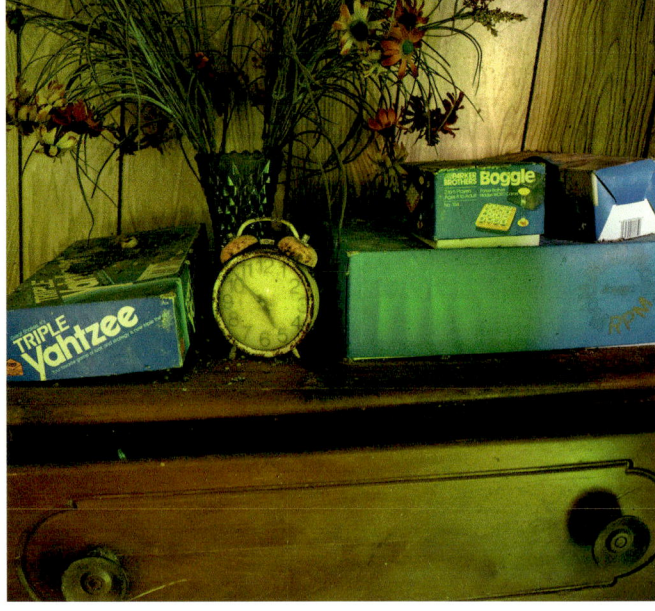

Above left: An old dresser sits mostly unscathed in a corner of the room, decorated with a green glass vase full of artificial flowers. A vintage alarm clock rests face-down between several board games.

Above right: Standing up the alarm clock reveals it wound down at 5:52 one day long ago.

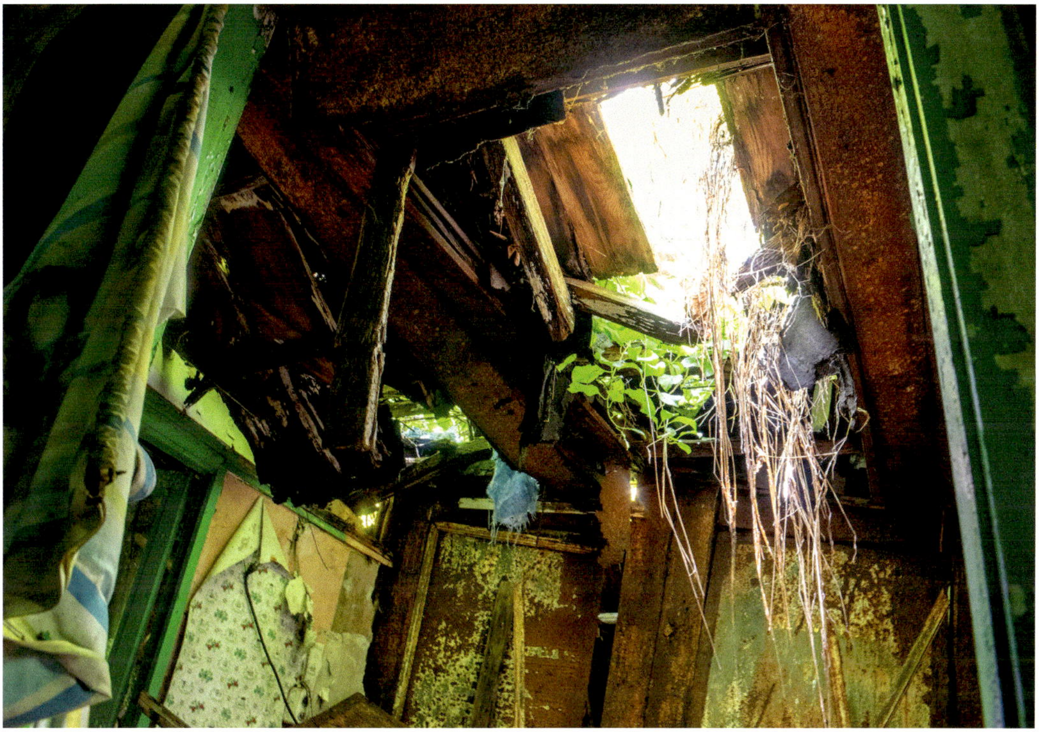

The ceiling in the back room has begun to fall apart, allowing an invasion of overgrowth.

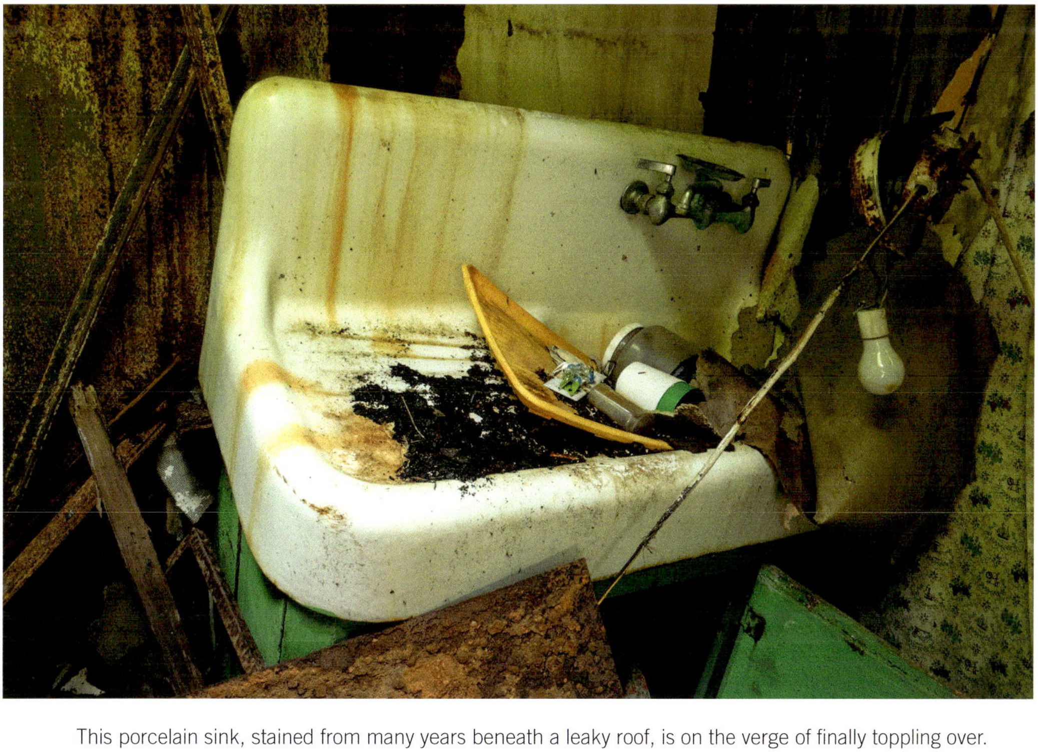

This porcelain sink, stained from many years beneath a leaky roof, is on the verge of finally toppling over.

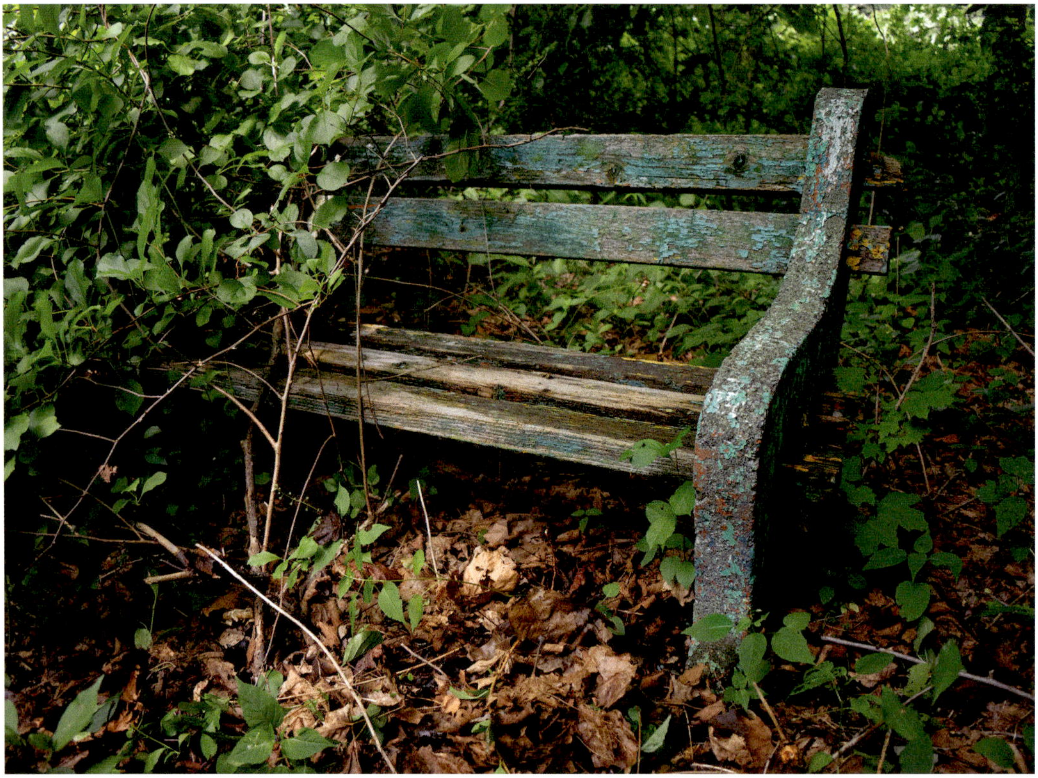

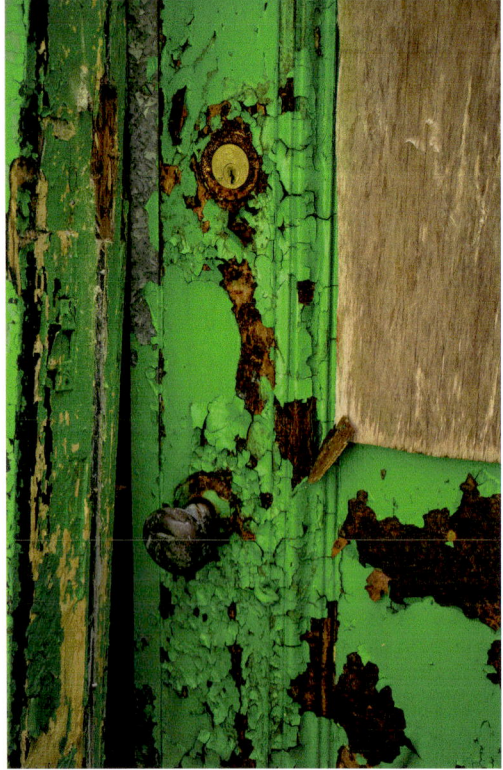

Above: A wooden bench faces the front of the cabin, offering a comfortable place to rest and enjoy the trees. Traces of red, blue, and green tell its color history.

Left: The rich verdigris paint job on the side door may be decaying, but what remains has not lost its intensity.

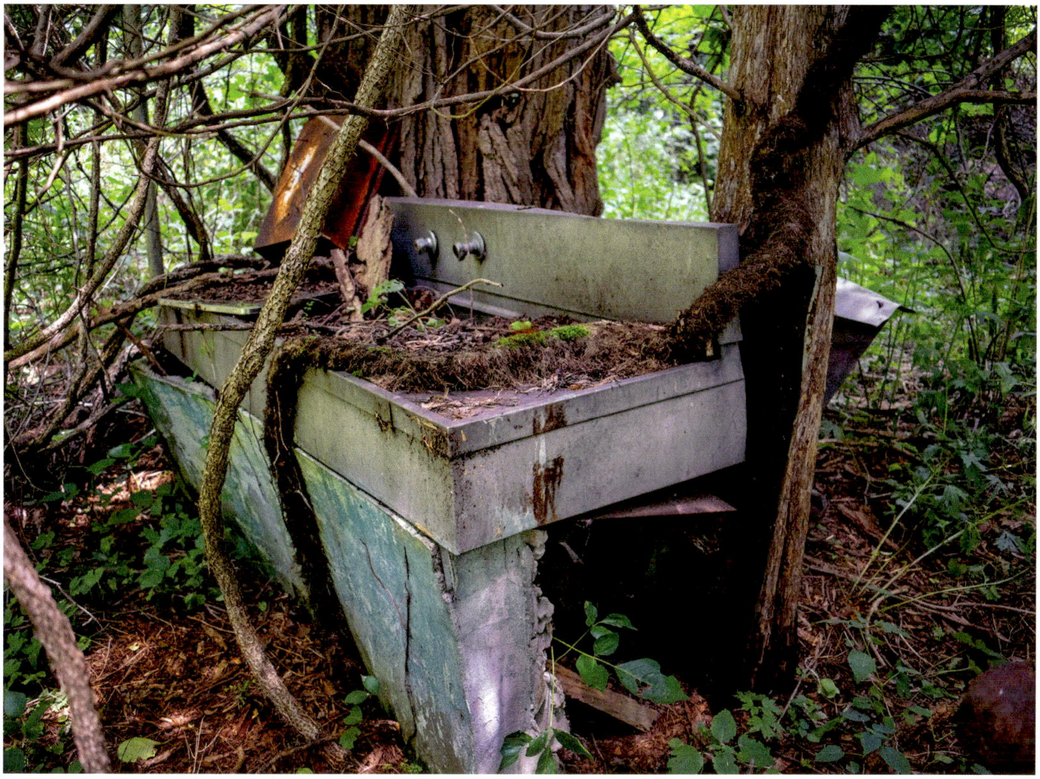

Above: A large utility sink has been pulled out and left to be enveloped by thick vines.

Right: An old outdoor thermometer still accurately registers the sweltering summer day.

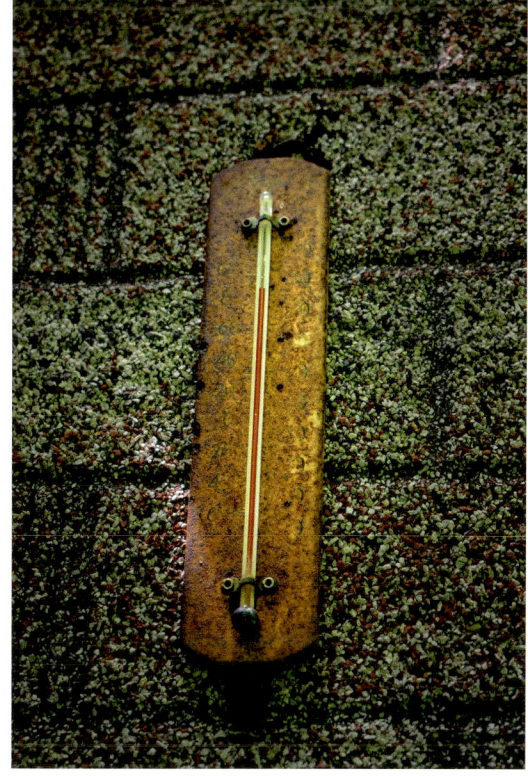

8

RURAL RELICS

A visit to Eastern Connecticut comes with an expectation of quaint villages, beautiful antique houses, picturesque farms, and innumerable stone walls that crisscross the landscape. But there is much more to discover if you make the effort. Abandoned and forgotten relics are everywhere here, from old silos and barns to derelict homes, churches, bridges, and other intriguing subjects. Some hide in plain sight, sitting on the outskirts of town, always there but never truly noticed. Many require luck and even the right season of the year to spot—elusive structures that only show themselves when the leaves have fallen, and you happen to be looking at just the right moment.

So, the next time you're in this part of the state, make a wrong turn. Shut down your GPS and see where the country roads take you. If you're paying attention to where you are and not where you're going, you might just uncover the bits and pieces of hidden history that elude the average day-tripper. With a little practice and patience, you'll become better and better at spotting these fascinating gems—venturing ever farther from your final destination, but closer to a past worth remembering.

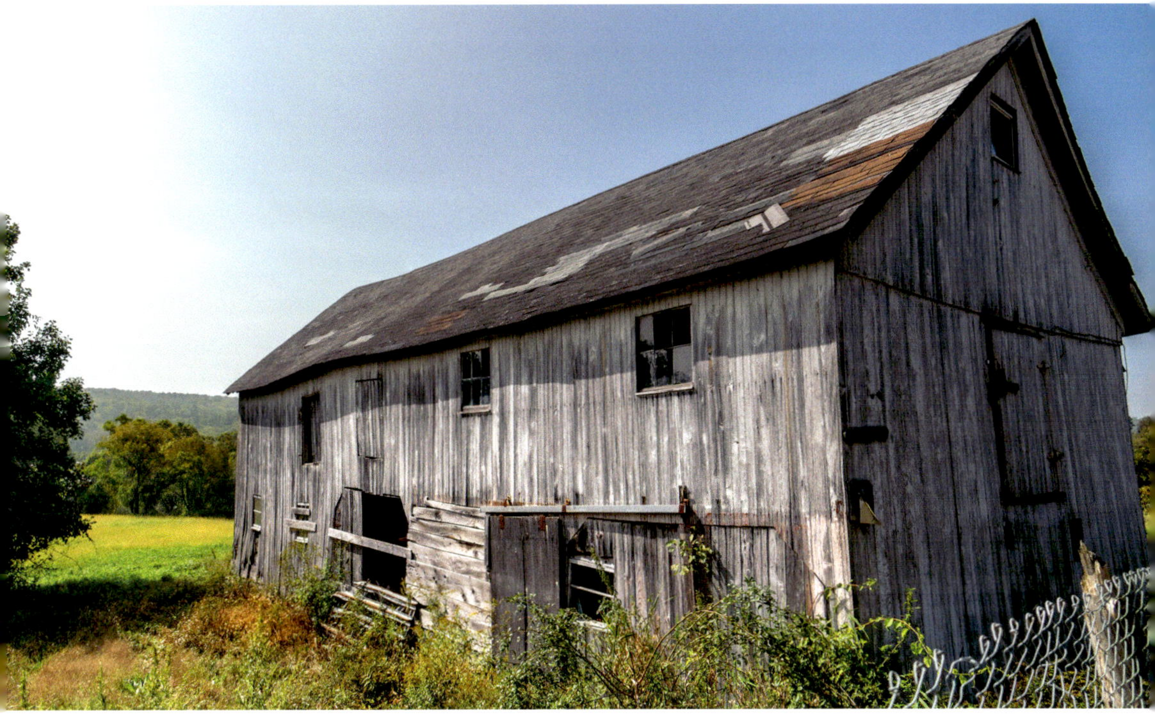

A rustic barn sits on the edge of beautiful Connecticut farmland.

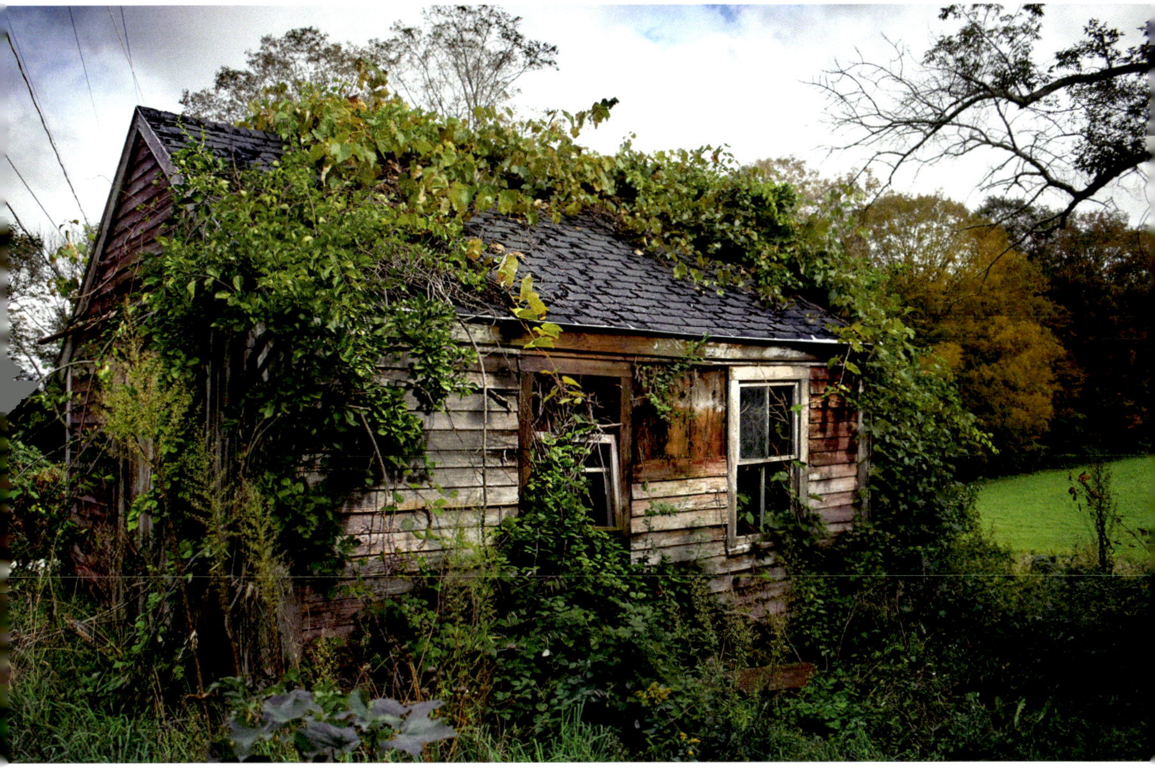

Sometimes, derelict buildings like this farm shack seem made for the moment you photograph them.

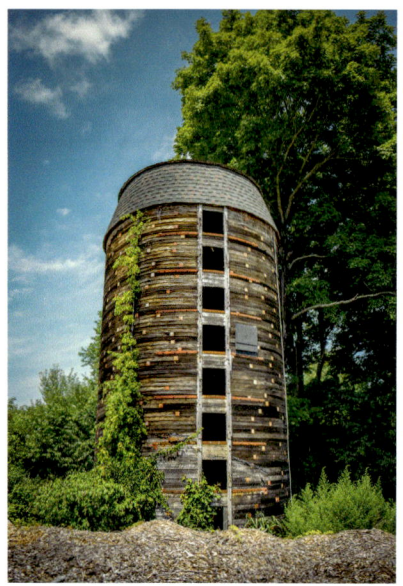 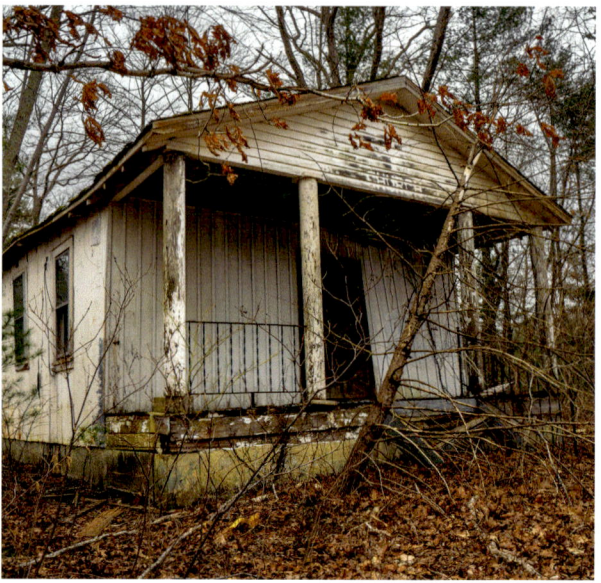

Above left: An old wooden silo is all that remains of a dairy farm once occupying land that is now a bird sanctuary.

Above right: This abandoned Baptist church, pictured in early spring, dates to 1969. The word "Church" is still discernible where a sign on the pediment used to be.

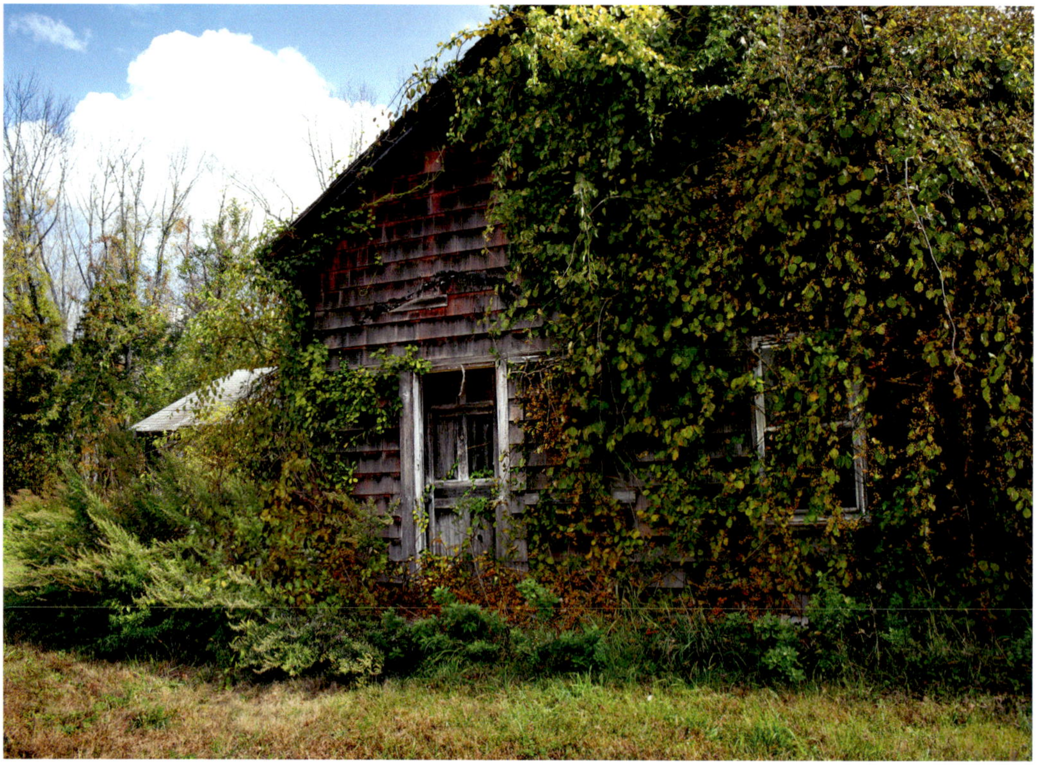

A quaint seventeenth-century house engulfed by ivy and weeds, closing in on the point of no return. Ironically, it was last occupied by a real estate office.

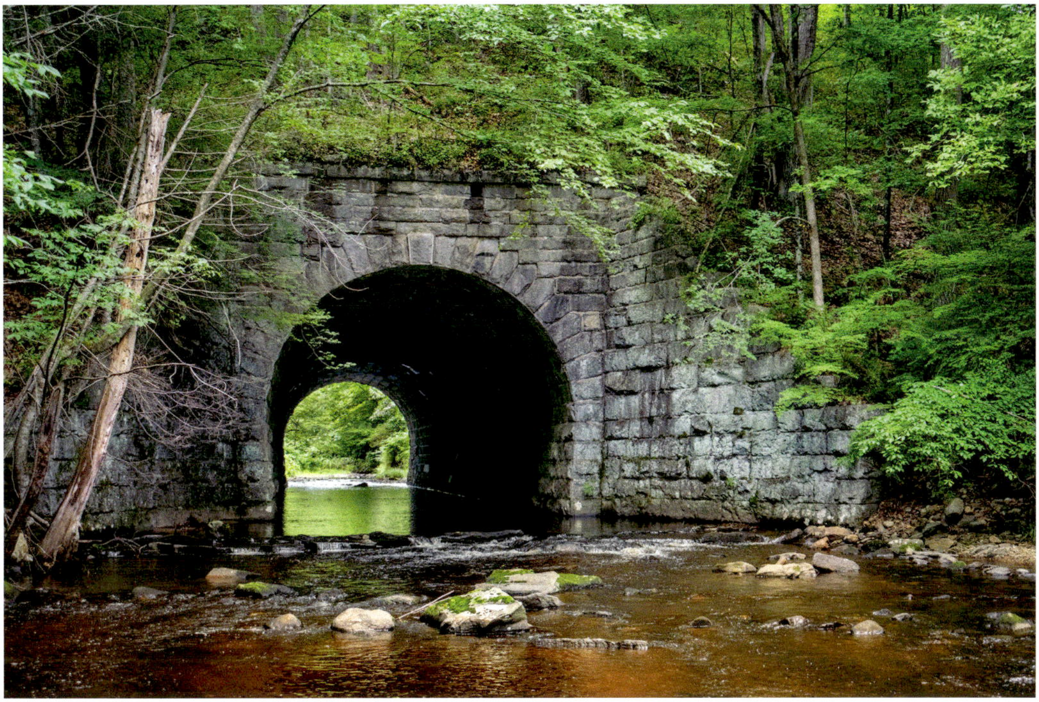

The ill-fated Air Line Railroad, an express service connecting Boston and New York, once ran across this Victorian-era arched bridge, one of many that span streams along the route. Today, it supports a multi-use public trail created from the old track bed.

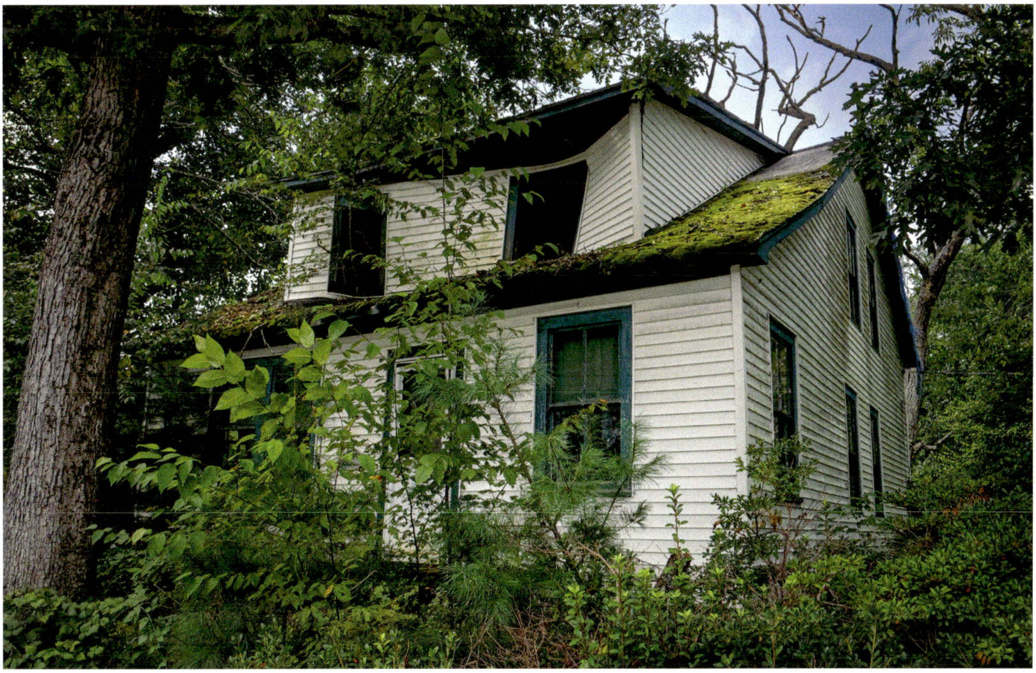

An early 1900s farmhouse slowly collapses beside a country road.

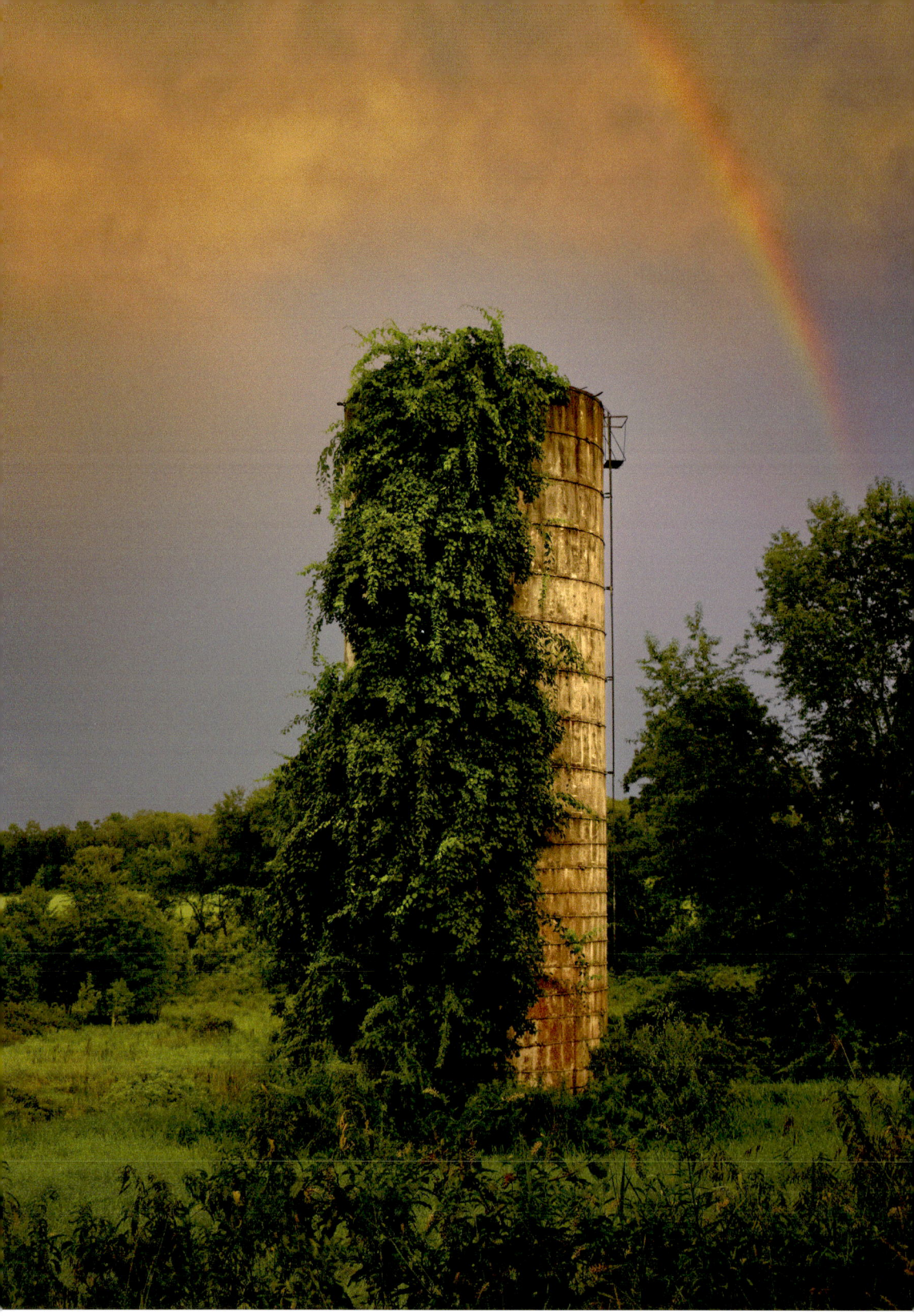

A picturesque farm silo at sunset, photographed after a thunderstorm left behind a golden sky with lovely rainbow.

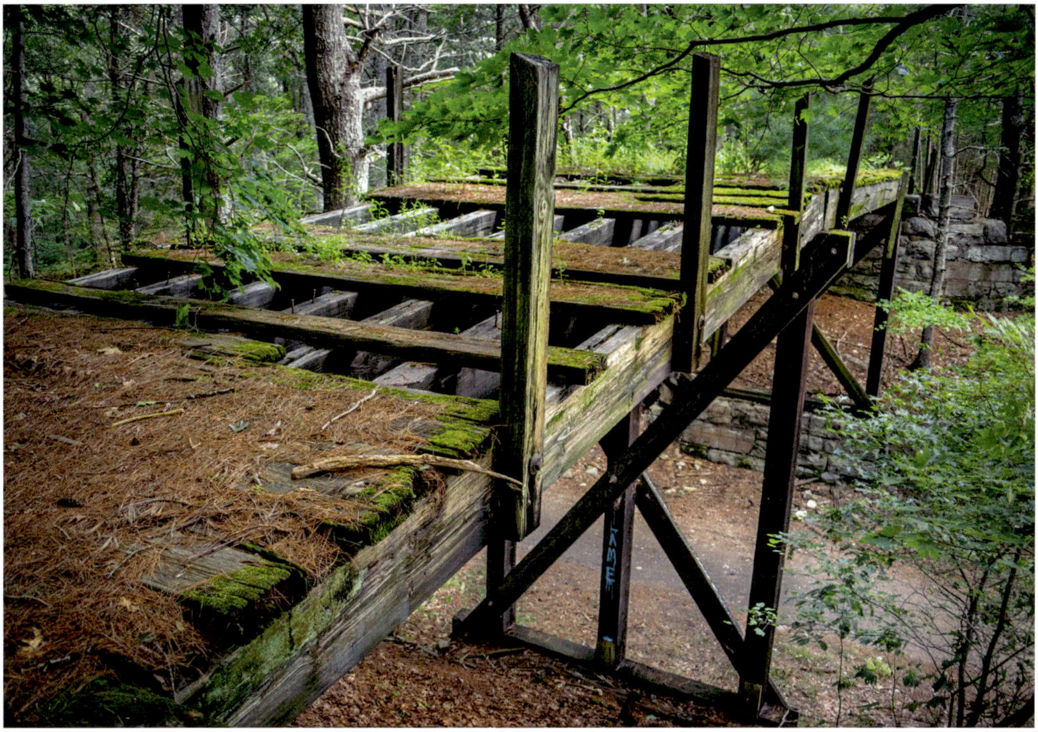

A view across the Air Line Trail cattle bridge. This wooden structure was built to allow farmers to safely cross their livestock without fear of oncoming trains—now replaced with casual hikers.

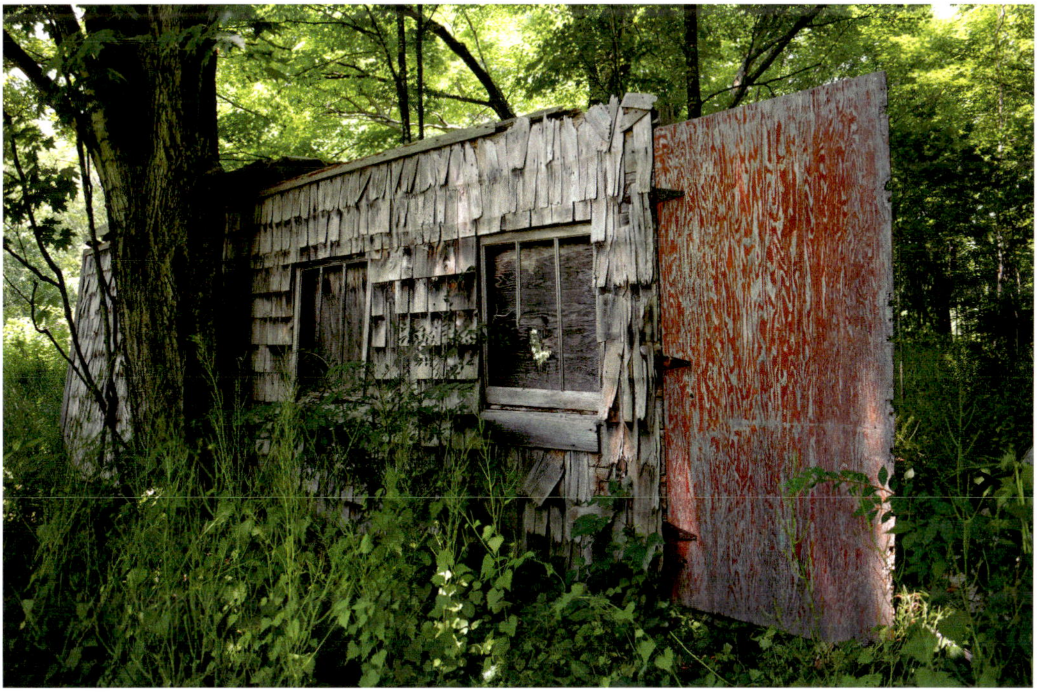

The façade of this hollowed-out fishing shack brings to mind a false-front movie set.

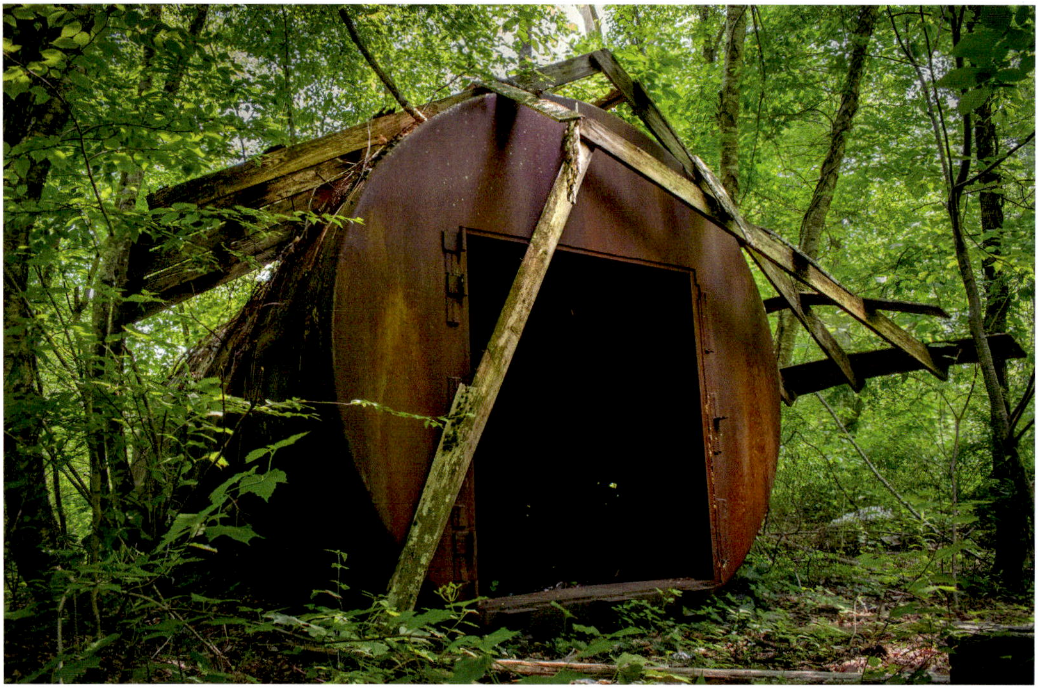

One of the strangest finds yet, this huge metal drum kiln with a makeshift roof once served in the production of charcoal sold by a small local business.

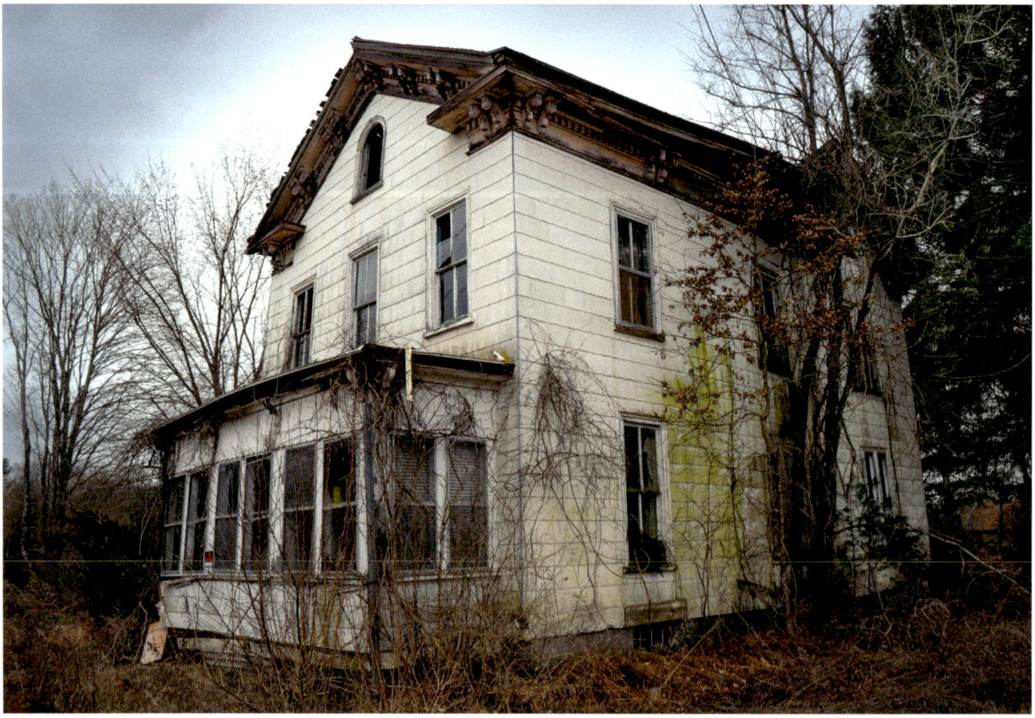

The ornate corbels and dentil trim on this abandoned 1920 farmhouse are still an impressive sight—products from an age of superior craftsmanship.

9

INDUSTRIAL ECHOES

The privilege of living in the Quiet Corner means being surrounded by abundant natural beauty. But beyond the serene imagery of rural Eastern Connecticut, there is another kind of aesthetic that is just as integral to the region's history. From as early as the eighteenth century, its waterways have been home to architecturally marvelous mills and factories that helped transform the New England economy and power a broader Industrial Revolution. And they can be found everywhere. From the colossal megastructures of the Victorian era to humbler examples of earlier times, their legacy remains a tangible presence even though many have gone permanently silent.

If you spend any time traveling through towns such as Norwich, Killingly, Thompson, or others with a strong industrial heritage, what's left of these once-thriving factories is hard to miss. Some have stubbornly withstood the threats of fires and natural disasters, their towers still proudly standing. More than a few have become literal shells of their former glory, victims of arson or brought low by decades of decay. However, even the most ruinous examples have something to offer—perhaps a lesson in period craftsmanship discernable in a half-crumbled wall, or a piece of old machinery that illustrates a manufacturing process, or just a simple foundation that outlines a place where determined people once labored to provide for their families.

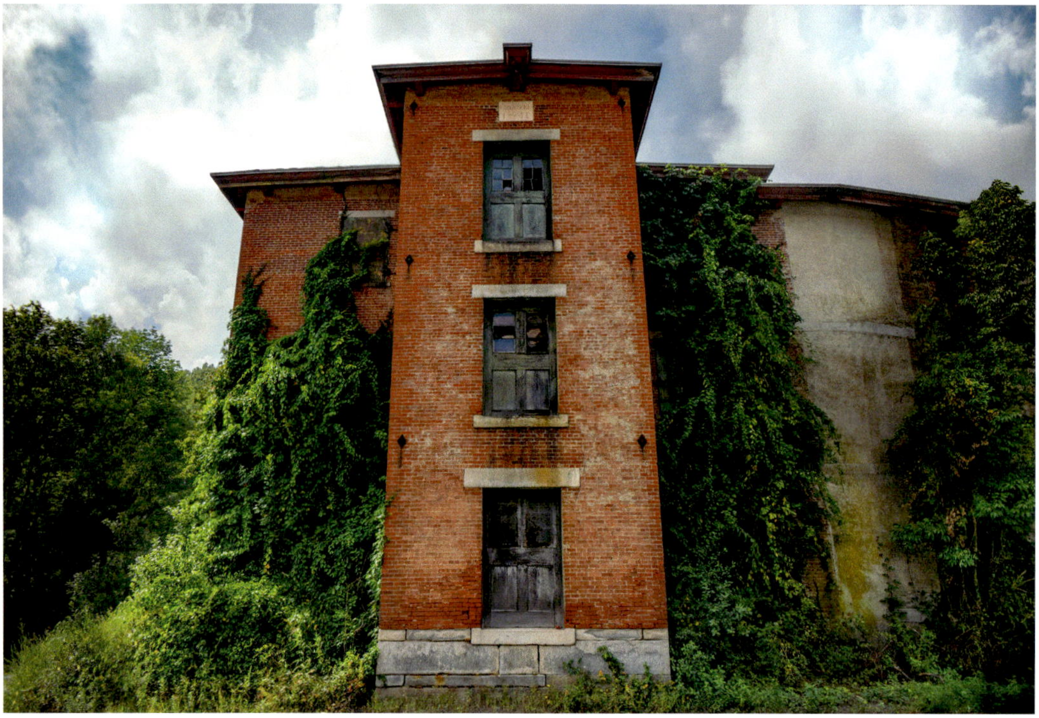

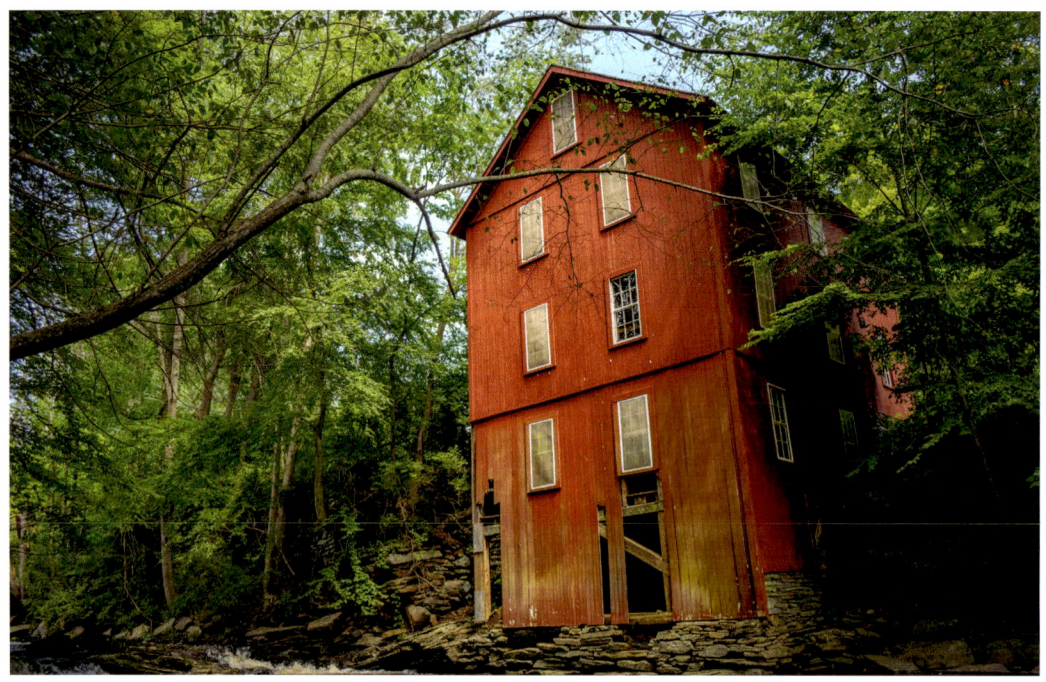

Historic Masonville Mills in Thompson. This 1826 building and its 1831 expansion added to the capacity of an original wooden mill specializing in fine cotton products. Unused for years, its last occupant was a plastics manufacturer.

Brayton Grist Mill in Pomfret's Mashamoquet Brook State Park. Built *c.* 1890 of salvaged materials, it is the lone survivor among a number of mill buildings that once lined the water here as early as 1816.

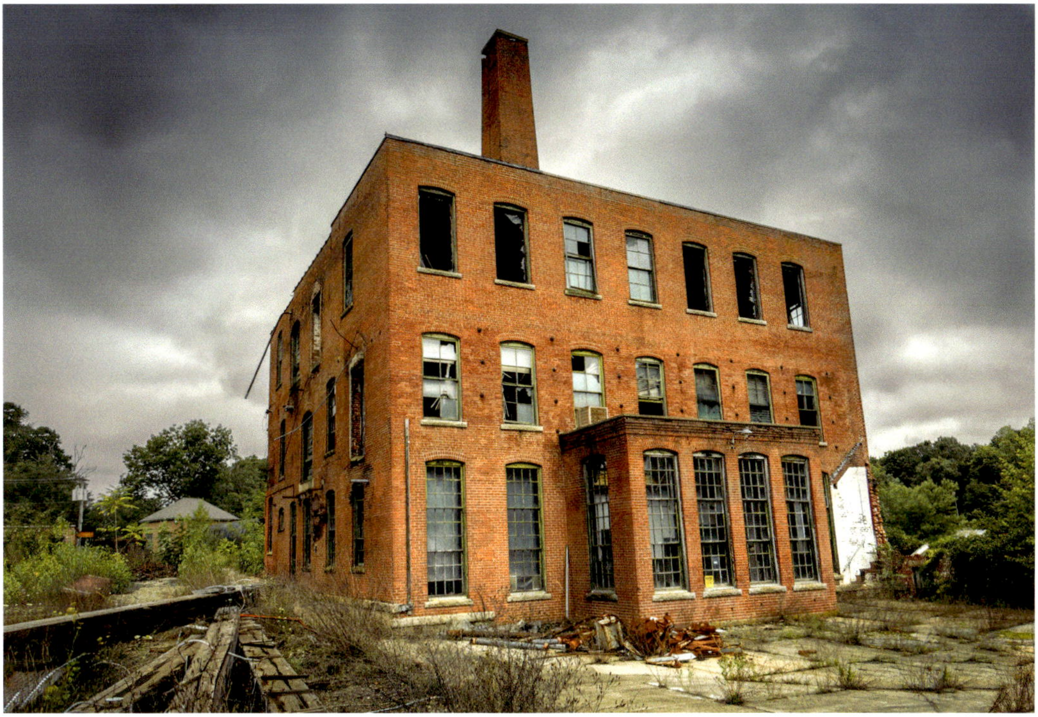

Dayville Mills in Killingly. The ruins of this 1882 woolen mill sit in the center of historic Dayville village. Noted for its pleasing architecture, it had been marked for redevelopment before a massive fire decimated the site in 2019.

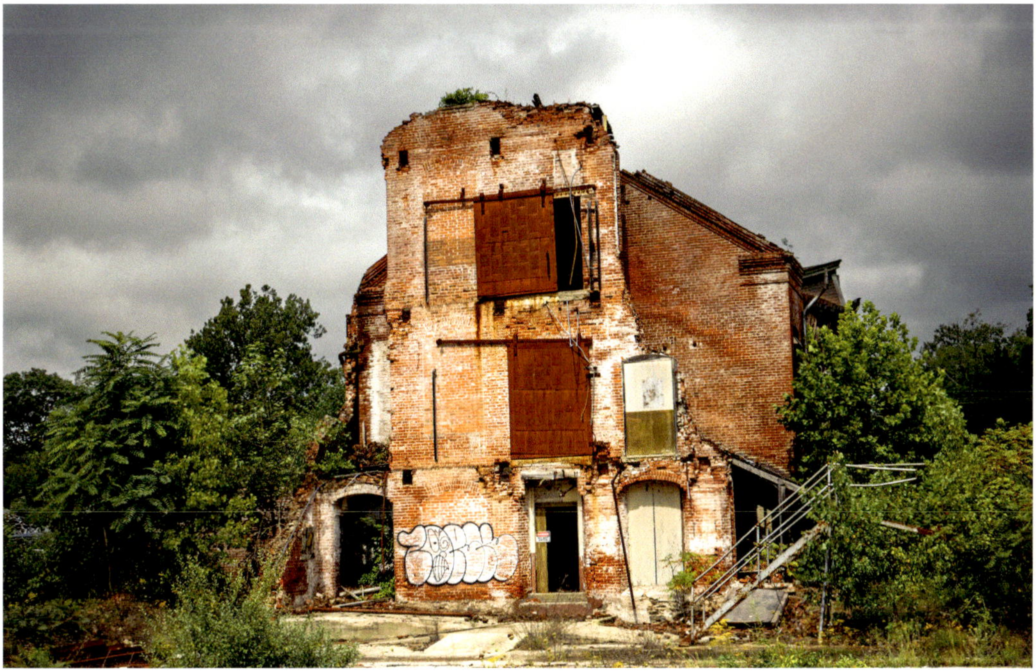

Another fire-destroyed building from the Dayville Mills complex looks like a post-war ruin.

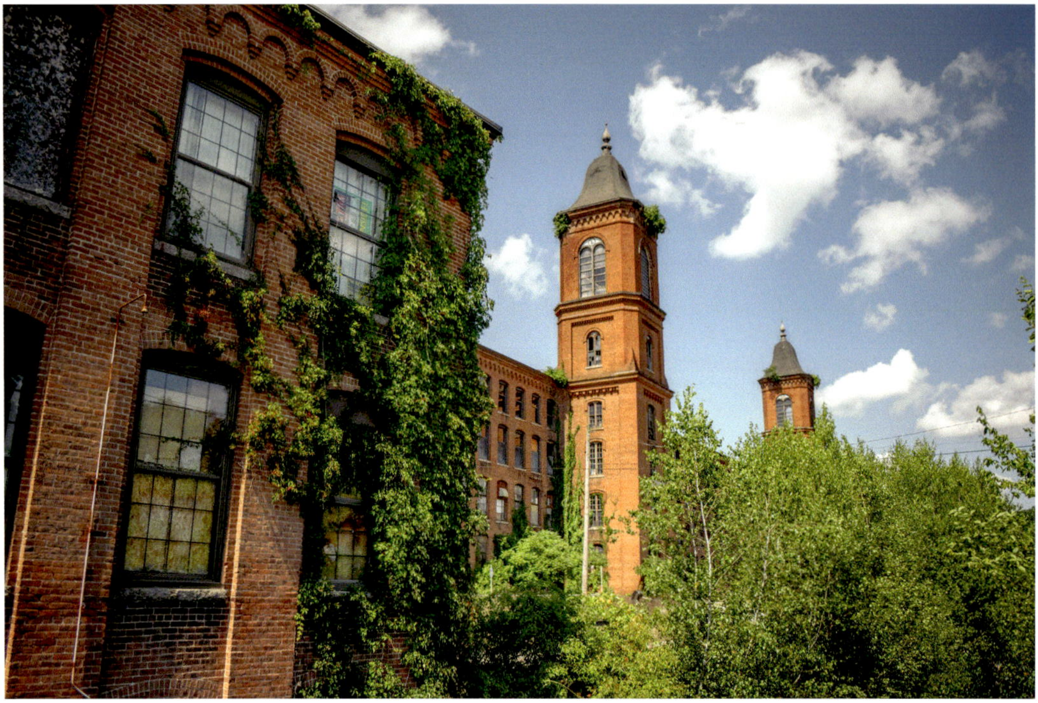

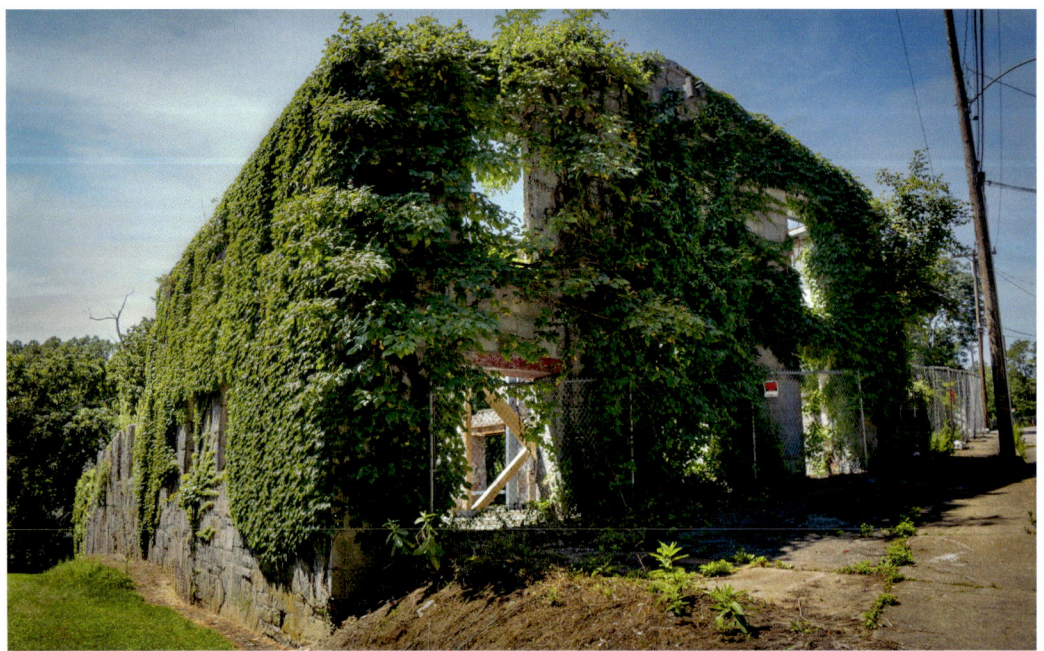

Thompson's North Grosvenordale Mill rises up along the French River like an industrial castle. Constructed in 1872, this abandoned cotton mill, one of the state's largest, occupies a 25-acre site that dominates the Grosvenordale village district.

The ruins of Falls Mill at Uncas Leap have been snatched from the jaws of demolition. Thanks to an ambitious project by the city of Norwich, the 1830 site has been incorporated into a new heritage park commemorating a legendary battle between the Mohegan and Narragansett tribes.

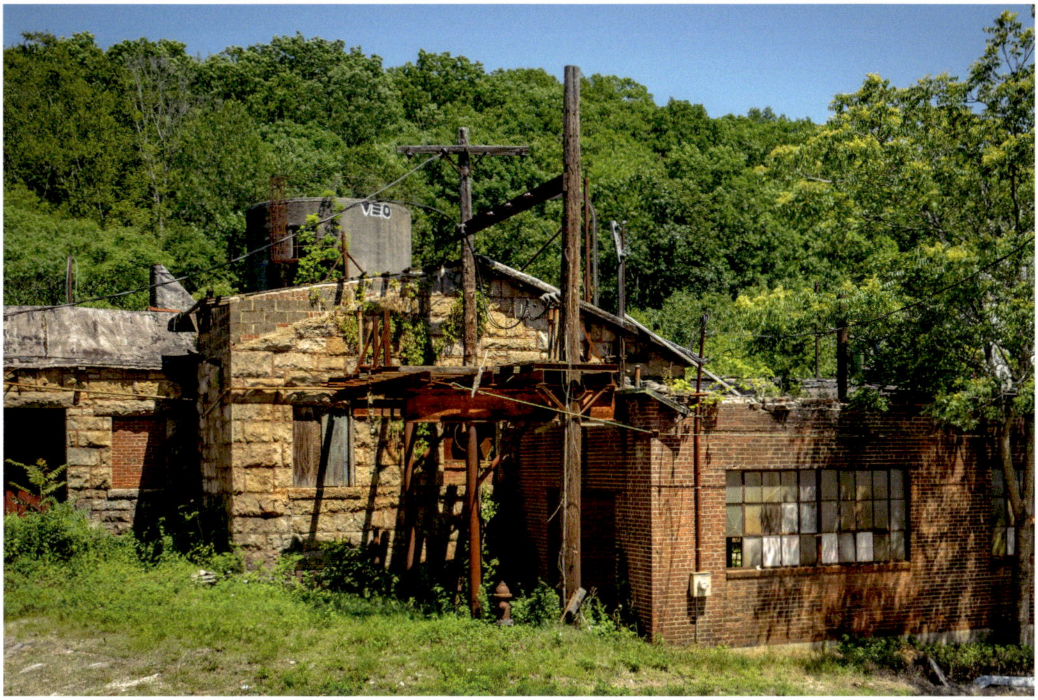

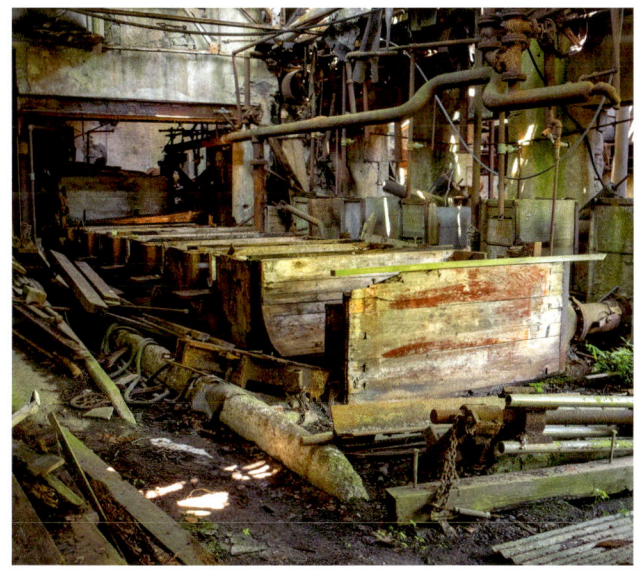

A small riverside paper mill features an original stone building dating to 1886 and several twentieth-century additions.

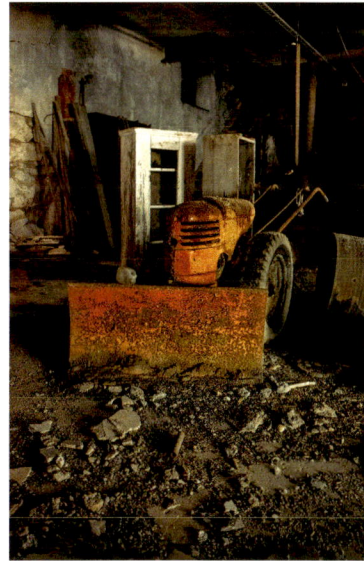

Above left: Manufacturing vats occupy one of this derelict paper mill's largest rooms.

Above right: A mid-century push-dozer found in an abandoned paper mill still looks almost serviceable.

10

CEMETERIES, LEGENDS, AND LORE

Israel Putnam and the Wolf Den

This cave in Pomfret was home to the last wolf in Connecticut, slain here in 1742. The she-wolf had killed a great number of livestock in preceding years and long evaded settlers who sought to take revenge. That is, until a young farmer named Israel Putnam rose to their defense. Israel, having lost many sheep himself, pursued the predator through the December snow for days until finally cornering her on an outcropping near Mashamoquet Brook. After it retreated into its den, a 20-foot-deep cave formed from a natural fissure, the only choice before him was to follow inside or return in defeat. As the story goes, with a torch in one hand and a musket in the other, he ventured into the wolf's rocky lair and ended its reign of terror once and for all. Putnam's waiting comrades, having tied a rope to his ankles, then pulled him back out while he dragged the animal's remains behind him.

In some ways, this is a sad outcome—a timeworn conflict between man and the natural world. For colonists living a tenuous existence, it was cause for celebration. They promptly threw a parade and feast, thereafter elevating Putnam to the status of a local hero and bestowing on him the nickname "Old Wolf Put." But his star would rise much further. Achieving wide-ranging success in early life, an older and wealthier Putnam was ultimately appointed as one of the highest-ranking generals of the revolution, serving directly under George Washington. However, a sudden illness forced him to retire before the war ended, and he returned to the Quiet Corner to tend to his business in peace.

Today, Putnam's legacy is evident in many places, from a town named in his honor to a Victorian-era monument in Brooklyn that depicts the general on horseback. More than just an impressive statue, it also serves as a second and final resting place. After his original grave had deteriorated to a degree unbefitting such a legendary citizen, the new tomb was commissioned, and Putnam was interred within. Sculpted wolf heads can be found on either side of the base in honor of his fabled history.

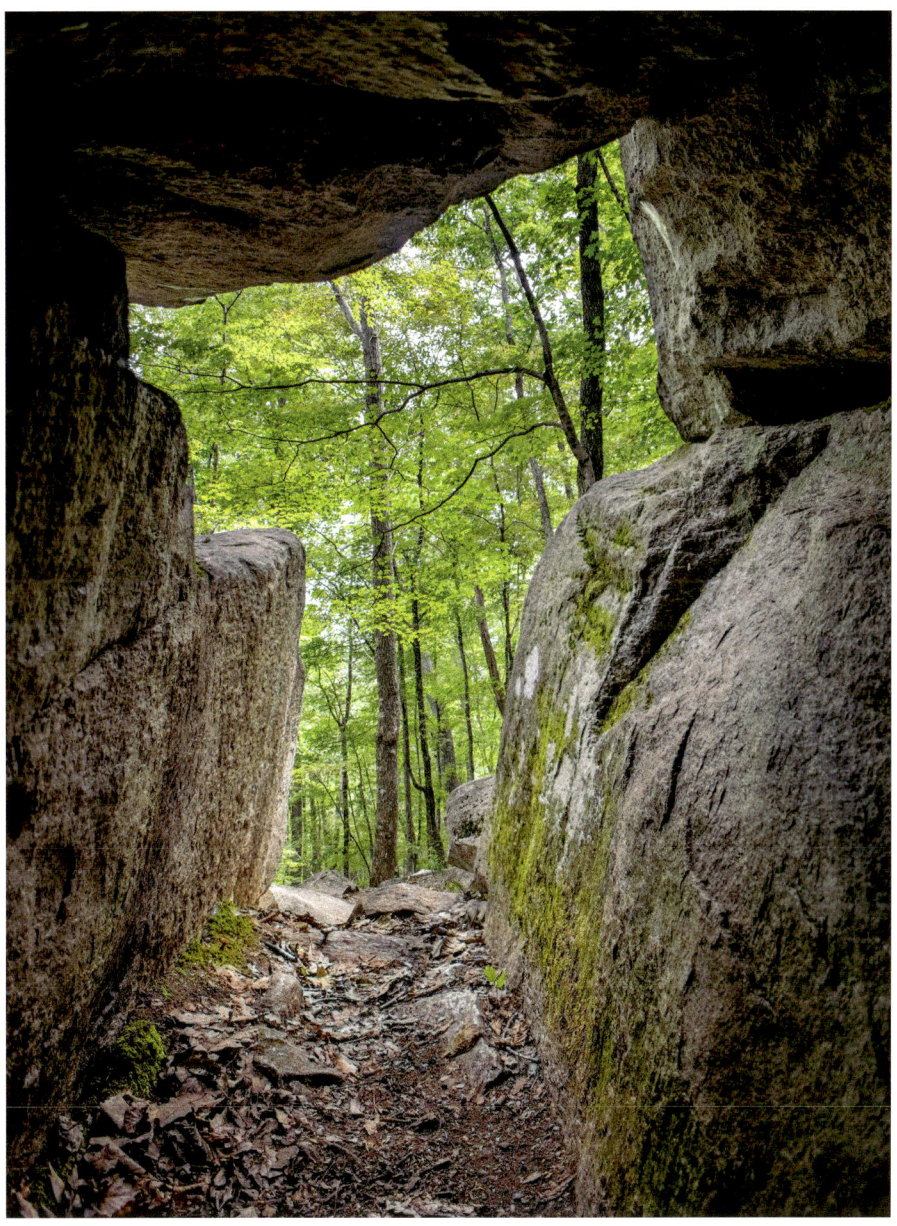

A view looking out from the 20-foot-deep cave, formed from a natural fissure in a ledge of gneiss rock.

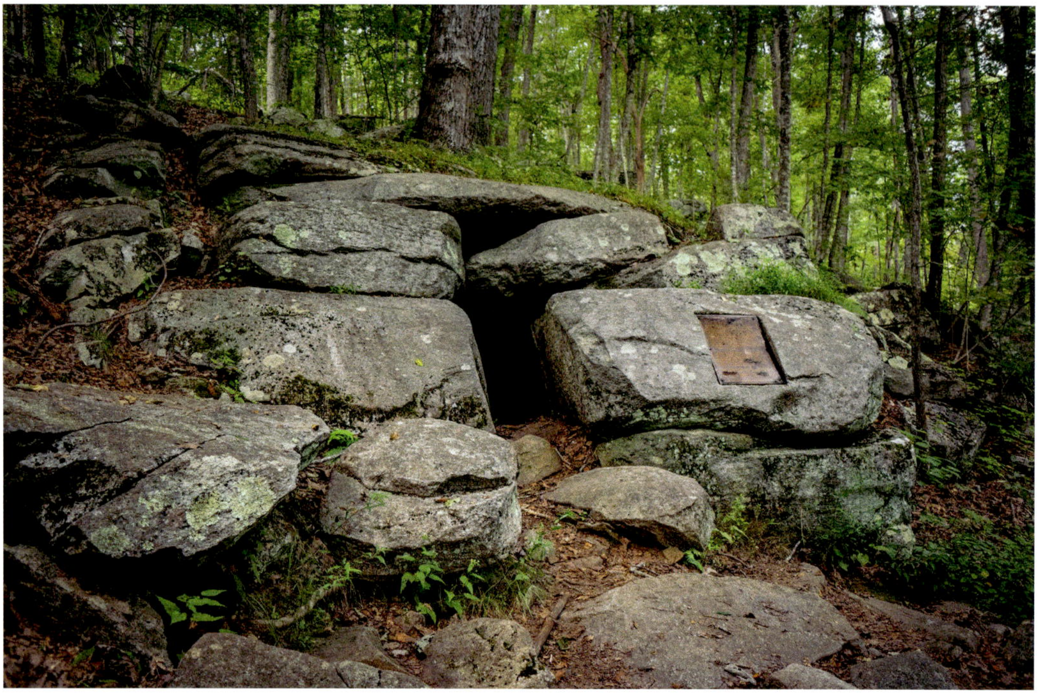

The last known wolf in Connecticut was killed here in 1742. Located in Mashamoquet Brook State Park, the Israel Putnam Wolf Den is listed on the National Register of Historic Places.

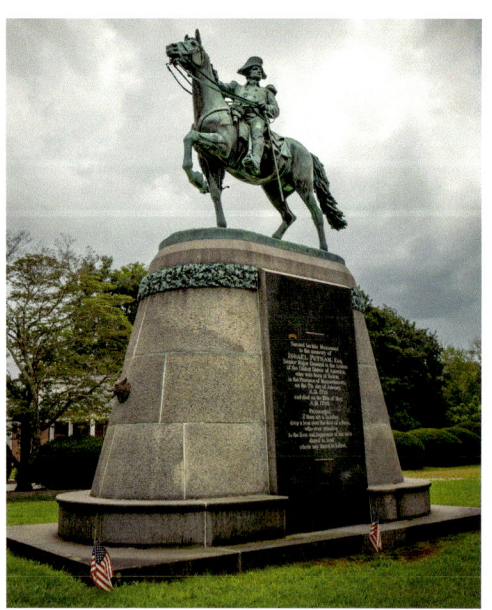

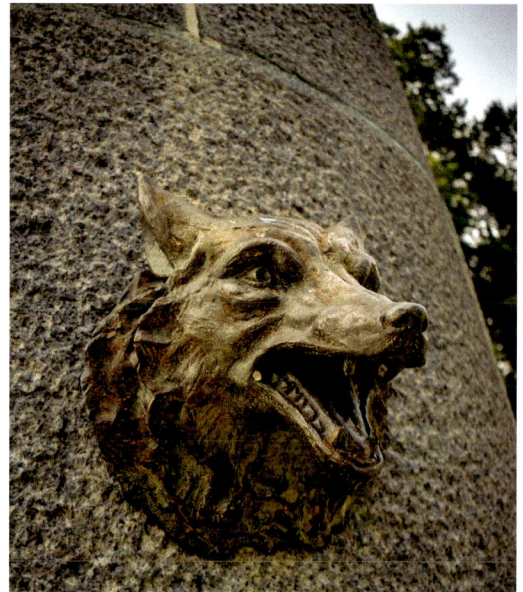

Above left: "The patriot who sleeps beneath this marble." In 1886, controversy over the deterioration of Putnam's original grave prompted the commission of the Israel Putnam Monument, which stands near the center of Brooklyn. Once completed in 1888, his remains were exhumed from a nearby cemetery and interred within its base.

Above right: Each side of the Israel Putnam Monument features a sculpted wolf head in honor of his legendary history.

The Oneco Stone Chamber

Is the Oneco Stone Chamber evidence that Vikings settled in New England? This simple yet well-constructed shelter found in Oneco's pine barren forest is one of a number of similar buildings throughout the region with origins that remain a mystery. Some believe they were the work of pre-Columbian Europeans who arrived on the East Coast long before commonly believed. Others suggest they could be of Native American origin, or perhaps rustic root cellars created by early colonists whose histories are now forgotten. Perfectly preserved and artfully blended into a rolling hillside, the chamber is, at the very least, a masterpiece of stonework built to last.

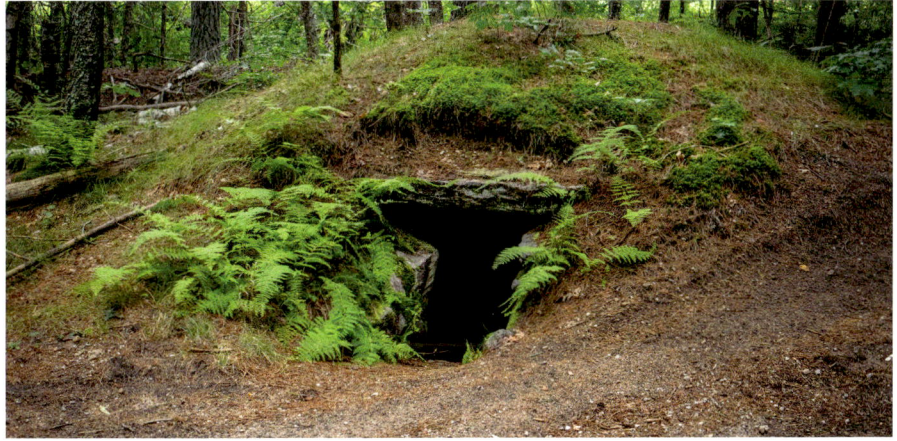

Above: The Oneco Stone Chamber can be found within a pine-barren forest in Oneco, a village of Sterling. Although many theories exist as to its origin and purpose, the truth remains uncertain.

Below: Perfectly intact stonework shows the skill of the chamber's builders, whoever they were.

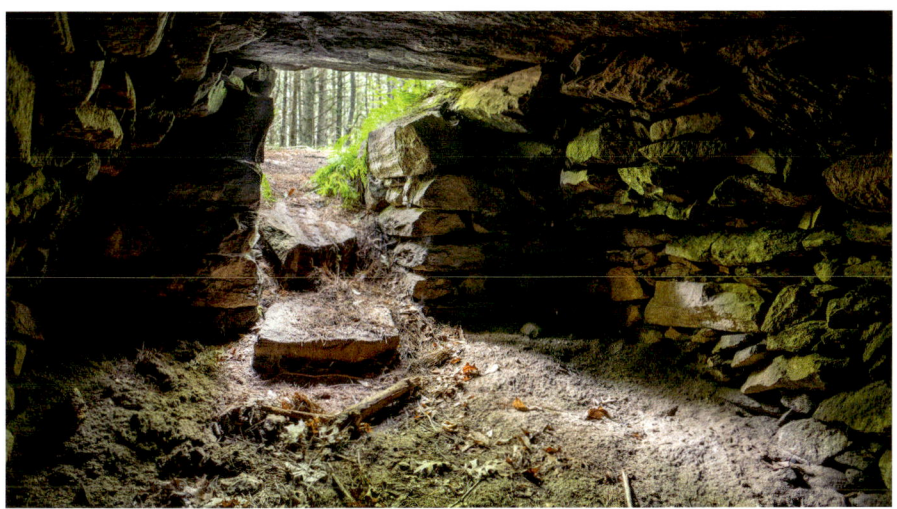

The Legend of Diana's Pool

Slipping on tears that soaked the rocks beneath her feet, lovelorn Diana plummeted to her death amid the icy churn of the falls below—or so legend says. Diana's Pool, a popular park in Chaplin, reputedly takes its name from the tale of a jilted young woman—the victim of a romantic affair gone wrong. In her heartbreak, she wandered one night to the cliffs above the Natchaug River, where she met a tragic and untimely end. Some say she threw herself over in despair, some that she was pushed by an angry beau who had followed after. Whichever sad version of a "lover's leap" you prefer, visitors to this beautiful spot can reflect on Diana's fate while taking in the gorgeous waterfalls, historic bridge, and many scenic trails. And, just maybe, encounter her sobbing ghost on a moonlit evening.

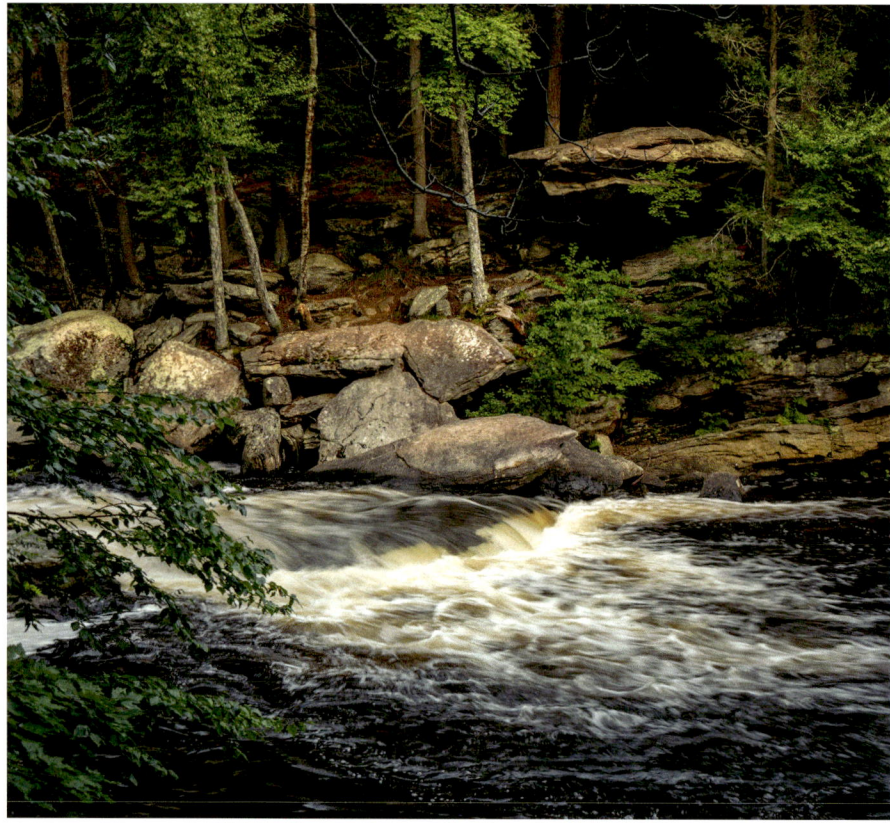

Diana's Pool is known for its beautiful but dangerous waterfalls. Many drownings have occurred here over the years, leading to a modern ban on swimming. It is easy to understand how a "lover's leap" legend might have evolved in such a romantic yet deadly spot. This long-exposure photograph illustrates the powerful flow of water.

The Blue Lady of Yantic Cemetery

What will the Blue Lady of Yantic Cemetery hold in her hands when you visit? This mysterious bronze statue, possibly of the Virgin Mary, has watched over the resting place of Sarah Larned for more than 130 years. Commissioned by Sarah's prominent Norwich family, the sculpture was created by renowned Victorian-era artist U. S. J. Dunbar in Washington, D.C., and cast in Philadelphia before being brought to the gravesite.

Admirers swear they've seen the Blue Lady clutching a rose, sometimes a Bible, rosary, or other object of veneration. These reports have inspired offerings of coins and mementos left beneath her mournful gaze, perhaps to petition her prayers and intervention in earthly matters. In a burial ground filled with extravagant monuments to the area's wealthiest people, the life-sized figure of this shrouded woman is by far the most famous. Whether inhabited by a spirit, an angel, or some other paranormal force, her otherworldly beauty is undeniable.

In 2010, the Blue Lady suffered severe vandalism, being kidnapped, dismantled, and her pieces scattered. Amazingly, the components were all recovered, the perpetrators brought to justice, and the statue restored by the city of Norwich within a year. Now, a new chapter of her vigil continues—this time behind the safety of a locked fence.

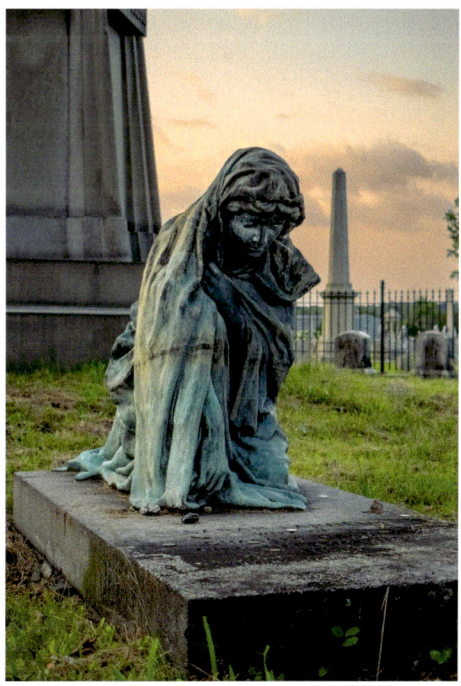

The Blue Lady of Yantic Cemetery has watched over the grave of Sarah Larned for more than 130 years. Some have reported her clutching various objects, including a rose and a Bible.

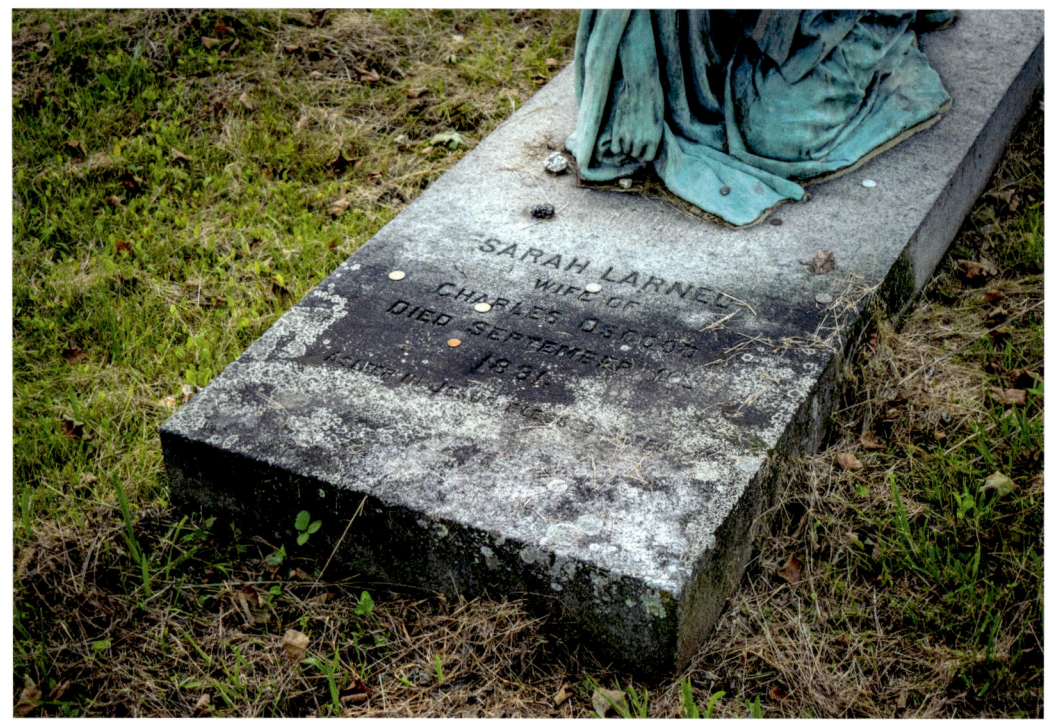

Reports of supernatural activity have inspired offerings of coins and mementos left on top of the grave marker.

The Jewett City Vampires

Exhumed and burned in front of their own graves, members of the Ray family of Jewett City were among the many posthumous victims of the Great New England Vampire Panic. During the nineteenth century, some populations of Connecticut, Rhode Island, and Massachusetts attributed outbreaks of consumption to the work of the undead. Having beaten the odds of the day by raising five healthy children to adulthood, the Rays seemed to be blessed with an enviable resilience—but their luck would not last much longer. When two young brothers, Lemuel and Elisha, and their father, Henry, all became afflicted with tuberculosis, the family's fortunes took a frightening turn. Suffering a slow, "consuming" death, they seemed to waste away as though preyed on by supernatural forces.

When a third son, Henry Jr., became sick as well, the surviving Rays resorted to drastic action. As tradition taught them, these signs of continuous persecution pointed to vampirism—and a shocking conclusion that their deceased relations, once stricken themselves, must be rising from the cemetery at night to feed on

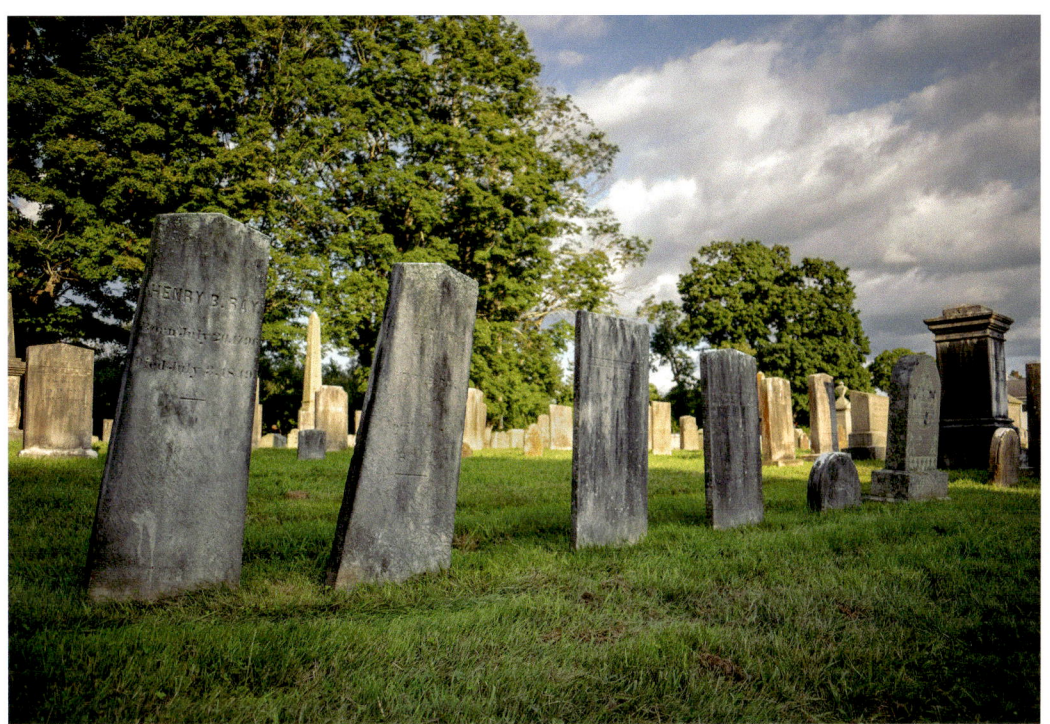

A row of Ray family graves in Jewett City Cemetery has become a notorious location associated with The Great New England Vampire Panic. Here the decomposing bodies of two young brothers, Lemuel and Elisha, were dug up and set ablaze before their own headstones. From left to right: Henry B. Ray, Lucy H. Ray, Lemuel B. Ray, and Elisha H. Ray.

the living. According to the beliefs of the era, destroying their corpses was the only surefire way to put an end to this terror. Incredibly, the remaining Rays dug the bodies of brothers Lemuel and Elisha from the earth and set fire to them "on the spot," as reported by a local newspaper. For them, unlike many others who followed this horrifying ritual, it was believed a success. Henry Jr. recovered from his illness, and the remaining family lived on.

Old Trinity Church

Is this perhaps the most haunted church in Connecticut? Tales abound of frequent paranormal activity at Brooklyn's Old Trinity Church, often involving sightings of the young victims of infamous serial killer Michael Ross. His heinous crime spree, conducted during the early 1980s, targeted eight local schoolgirls and women before

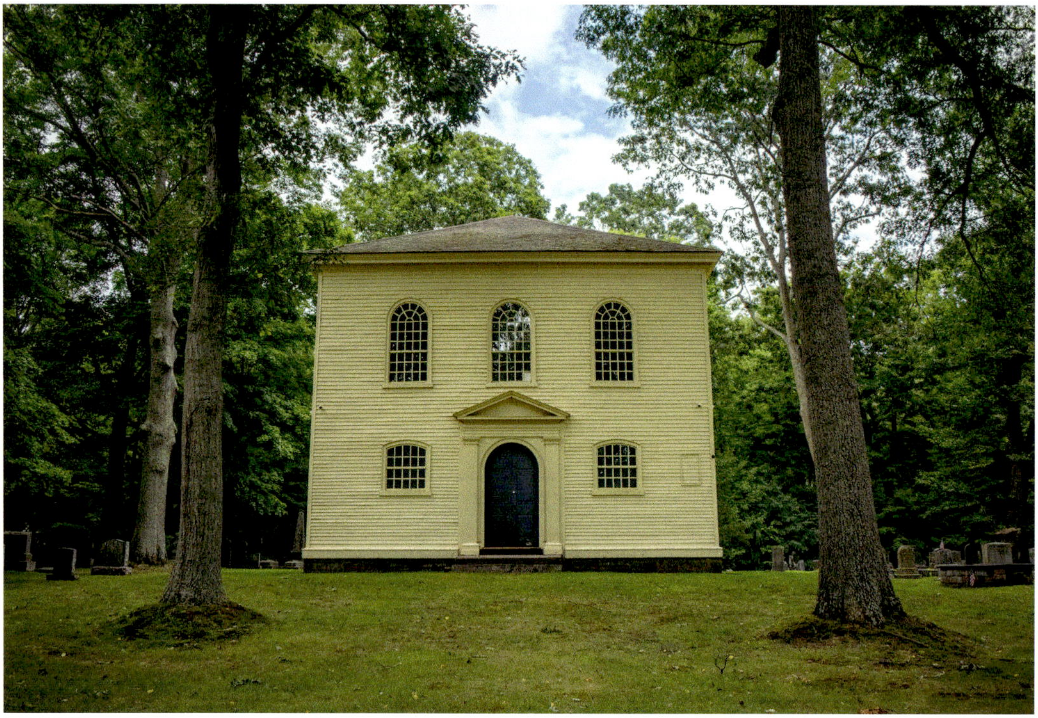

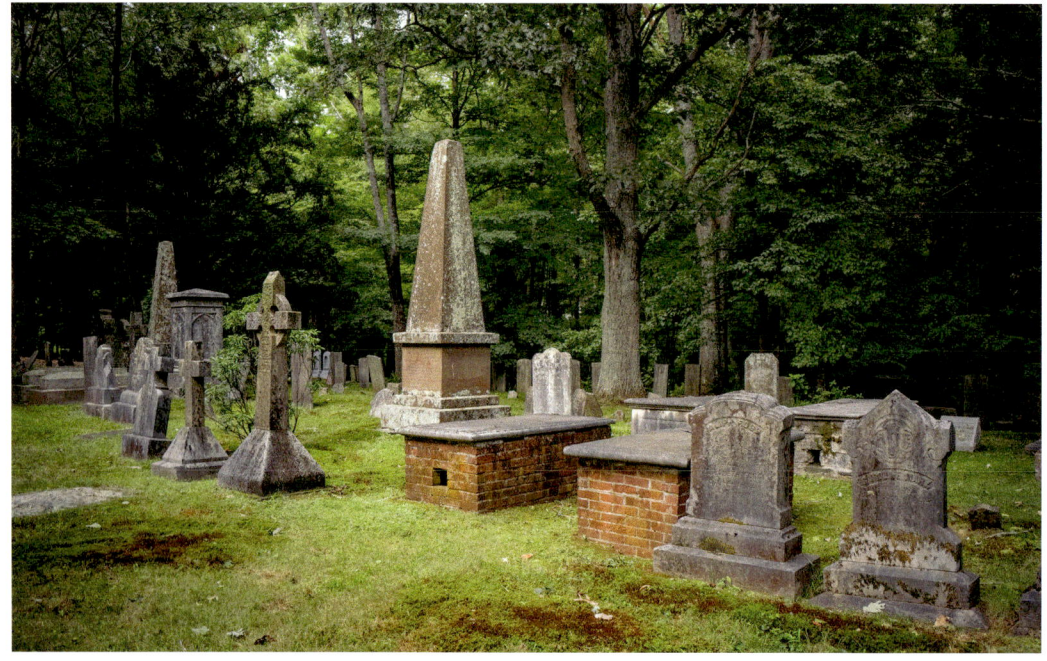

Old Trinity is the oldest surviving Anglican church in the state, built by royalist Godfrey Malbone to avoid paying taxes toward Brooklyn's construction of a new Episcopalian church. Dating to 1771, its haunted reputation and association with the Michael Ross murders exist alongside its significance as an architectural and historical landmark.

The burying ground at Old Trinity Church is both serenely beautiful and a history lesson on the area's oldest families.

he was finally apprehended. One of the deceased was reportedly found near a stone wall opposite Trinity's grounds, more than two years after her disappearance while walking along nearby Church Street (the precise spot is still a point of some debate).

Although its proximity to this horrible history has fostered Old Trinity's reputation as a haunted location, sightings of apparitions, orbs, and other phenomena long predate these events. Tradition also states that jumping the churchyard wall will result in a terrible curse, with few brave souls daring to test this outcome for themselves. Whether you're a believer or not, a visit will include a remarkably idyllic and well-preserved eighteenth-century meetinghouse, surrounded by a picturesque graveyard filled with many of the area's prominent families.

Trinity is the oldest-surviving Anglican church in the state, established by royalist Godfrey Malbone, who provided both money—and slave labor—toward its construction. His desire to avoid paying taxes to build an Episcopalian church in the center of town drove him to complete a new Anglican meetinghouse before this plan came to fruition. Designed by Malbone himself, the architecture adheres to a rigid cubist form along the lines of other New England examples of the time. Dating to 1771, this Brooklyn landmark is listed on the National Register of Historic Places.

The Abandoned Crypt

Can a tomb still feel haunted even though it was never used? Little is known about this abandoned nineteenth-century crypt in the woods of Northeastern Connecticut. Once thought to be a mere root cellar, it has since been attributed as the intended burial chamber of wealthy farmers, the details of their lives now lost. According to the local historical society, a document from 1837 attests that this "family tomb" was conveyed in an unfinished state along with the sale of the surrounding land. Whatever its origins, one thing is for certain: No one was ever actually interred here. Even so, a solitary visit on a gloomy day can be an unsettling experience. It's easy to imagine lingering spirits, perhaps of the original builders, waiting patiently for someone to come along and complete their forsaken resting place—or to make it your own.

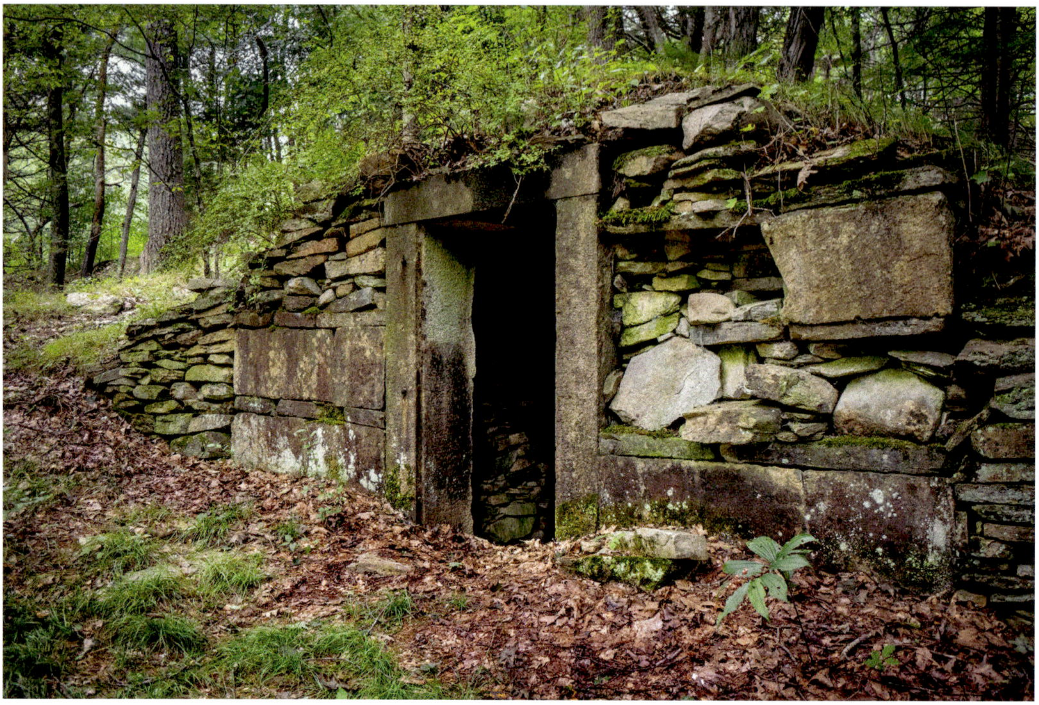

This abandoned family crypt in Northeastern Connecticut was reputedly built by wealthy Victorian farmers. Many of its finer blocks were likely removed for other uses and replaced with rough fieldstone.

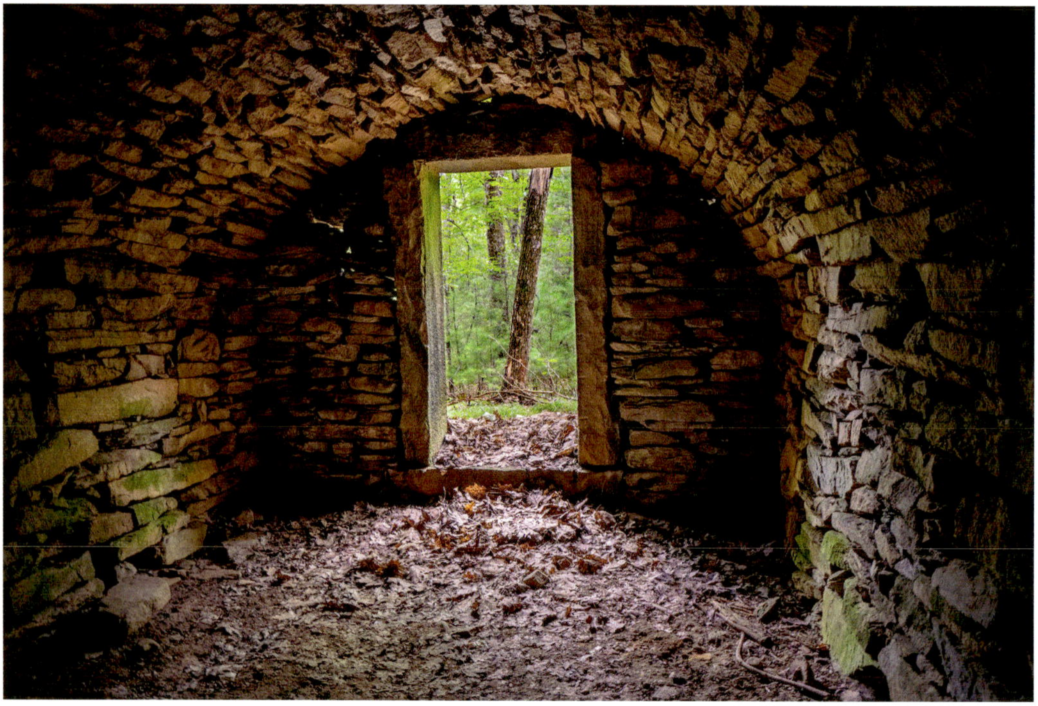

The interior of the chamber, with its corbelled gothic arch, exudes a haunting atmosphere despite never receiving any burials.

REFERENCES

Atlasobscura.com

Connecticutmills.org

Ct.gov

Damnedct.com

Epa.gov

Nawrocki, A., and Lehman, E., "The Rise and Fall of Connecticut Dairy Farming,"
    Ediblenutmeg.com

Norwichct.org

Silo.org

Taylor, B., "Connecticut's Farms are Dwindling," Wtnh.com

Thelastgreenvalley.org

Wikipedia.com

ABOUT THE AUTHOR

Designer and photographer Matthew Means has explored New England's hidden beauty and architectural heritage for over fifteen years. Under the moniker "Ghost of New England," he creates and publishes content that showcases the region's abandoned places and fascinating local history. From old industrial sites to derelict farms and moss-covered graveyards, his mission seeks to uncover a world of dusty gems and hidden treasures before they are lost forever. With a passion for historic preservation, Matthew has also embarked on the restoration of an eighteenth-century farm while continuing his journey to document endangered and forgotten locations through photography.

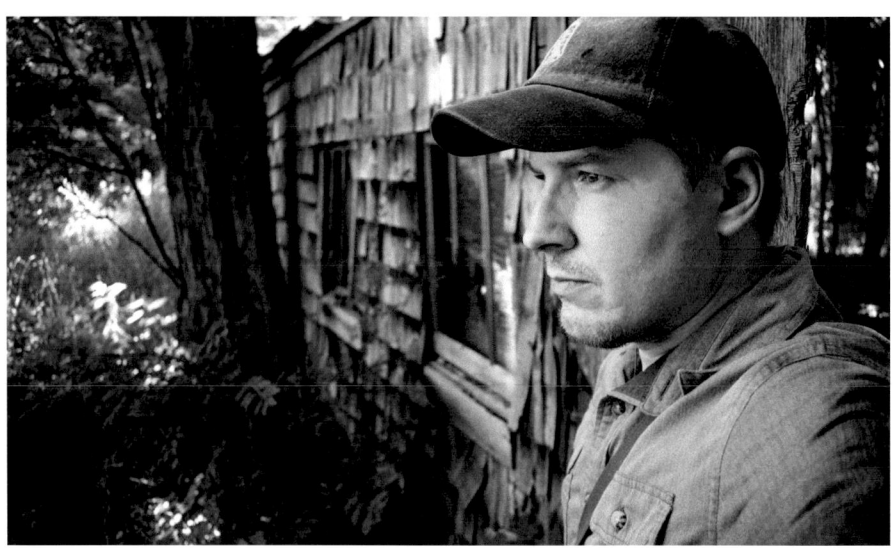